The
KIDS' FAMILY TREE
Book

The KIDS' FAMILY TREE Book

Caroline Leavitt

STERLING CHILDREN'S BOOKS
New York

Special thanks are due to all those—family and friends—who provided information and gave permission for the use of many old and perhaps slightly more recent photographs in this book. Your help was invaluable.

STERLING CHILDREN'S BOOKS
New York

An Imprint of Sterling Publishing Co., Inc.
1166 Avenue of the Americas
New York, NY 10036

STERLING CHILDREN'S BOOKS and the distinctive Sterling
logo are registered trademarks of Sterling Publishing Co., Inc.

ISBN 978-1-4549-2320-6

Library of Congress Cataloging-in-Publication Data
Names: Leavitt, Caroline, author. | Phillips, Ian (Illustrator), illustrator.
Title: The kids' family tree book / Caroline Leavitt ; illustrated by Ian
     Phillips.
Description: [Updated edition] | New York, NY : Sterling Children's Books,
     2017.
Identifiers: LCCN 2017007165 | ISBN 9781454923206 (paperback)
Subjects: LCSH: Genealogy—Juvenile literature. | BISAC: JUVENILE NONFICTION
     / Family / General (see also headings under Social Issues). | JUVENILE
     NONFICTION / Reference / General. | JUVENILE NONFICTION / Social Science /
     Customs, Traditions, Anthropology.
Classification: LCC CS15.5 .L43 2017 | DDC 929.2—dc23 LC record available at
     https://lccn.loc.gov/2017007165

Distributed in Canada by Sterling Publishing Co., Inc.
c/o Canadian Manda Group, 664 Annette Street
Toronto, Ontario, Canada M6S 2C8
Distributed in the United Kingdom by GMC Distribution Services
Castle Place, 166 High Street, Lewes, East Sussex, England BN7 1XU
Distributed in Australia by NewSouth Books
45 Beach Street, Coogee, NSW 2034, Australia

For information about custom editions, special sales, and premium and
corporate purchases, please contact Sterling Special Sales at 800-805-5489
or specialsales@sterlingpublishing.com.

Manufactured in China

Lot #:
2 4 6 8 10 9 7 5 3 1
07/17

sterlingpublishing.com

Illustrations by Jane Sanders
Design by Irene Vandervoort

Contents

Introduction

Do you have a family tree? No, don't look around for a big trunk topped with green leaves. That's not the kind of tree we're talking about. When you are born, you become a living and growing part of your own family tree. Your parents and brothers and sisters, and your aunts and uncles and other relatives, all play their parts in helping the branches of your family tree spread out and grow strong. Are you ready to put them in their honored places in your family tree? It's time to learn about and meet your ancestors. And it all begins with a word you may have heard: genealogy.

1

Genealogy Is You!

WHAT MAKES YOU YOU?

Ever wonder how you became who you are? Why you are tall or short? How your hair got to be curly or straight? Your skin dark or pale or olive?

How you got to be the way you are is due, in large part, to your family genealogy. Look at members of your family and you might notice things you all share, beyond the same last name and hometown. Your father might be tall the way you are and have the same springy dark hair. Your mother's brown eyes might be the same chocolate shade as yours. If you have siblings, maybe your brother has your same strong nose, or your sister shares your lopsided smile. If you are one of identical twins, it's like looking in a mirror!

It's not only "looks" that families share. Talents, such as a beautiful singing voice or being able to draw wonderful pictures, can also run in families. So can medical problems, such as being color-blind or sneezing when you're around cats or dogs or at certain times of the year. You might also be very different from your parents and siblings in some ways. Maybe you are short while they are all tall or you enjoy telling long involved stories, but your dad can't even tell a joke!

And then there's what you're like on the inside. Where do you get your personality? Do you like to sit quietly in a chair and read, lost for hours the way your mother does? Do you love the beach the way your cousins do? Or yearn to be a doctor like your dad? Are you more like your aunt than your mother? How so? Who shares what? Are there more people in your family who like to paint than who like to write? Who has the good sense of humor? Who is quick to anger? Do you have a temper, too? Has someone asked, "Who do you take after?" It's really a good question. Do you know the answer?

Knowing about your family can help you to learn a whole lot more about yourself. Knowing about your ancestors' place in their world can help you to understand your place in yours.

It's not all Mom and Dad

How you got to be you doesn't stop with just your immediate family. Maybe no one in your family now is tall like you, but maybe your great-uncle was six feet tall. And his father before him might have been six feet five! Of course, if you are adopted, you may not look anything like the family you know and love. You may have your birth mother's love of math or your birth father's flaming red hair.

Your family genes stretch far back, farther than anybody remembers. Think about it. Your mother had a mother, and her mother had a mother, and her mother had a mother, and her mother, too. Going back several generations, your great-grandfather's great-grandfather might have been a shoemaker in England. Your great-grandmother's great-grandmother might have been making lasagna in Italy or borscht (a tasty beet soup) in Russia. All these people could be a part of your family tree! And it's exciting to discover how these blood relations were like you, and how they were different.

Could this baby on her grandfather's knee be your great-grandmother?

It's always good to gather four generations together for a photo.

THE GENES IN YOUR JEANS

The important part of the word *genealogy*, which means the study of family history, is *gene*. Genes are the material in every cell of your body that give instructions to your body for creating the one and only special you. No one is exactly like you (only identical twins are the same, in terms of genetic material). Genes are carried on tiny structures called chromosomes. Every cell in your body has 46 chromosomes that come in pairs of 23 each.

Inside the chromosomes is your DNA (short for an expression that's a real mouthful: deoxyribonucleic acid), and this DNA is what gives your body the messages to create you.

You received your chromosomes—and your genes—from your parents: some from your father and some from your mother. Before you were born, your genes blended together and created a blueprint for the person you would be. Similarly, your parents got their genes from their parents (your mother from her mother and father, and your father from his mother and father). And those people, your grandparents, got their genes from your great-grandparents. I'm sure you can guess now where your great-grandparents got their genes. And aren't you getting excited about finally finding out just who all those people were and what they were like?

Genes dictate lots of things. Think of your extended family—your uncles, aunts, and grandparents. If they share the same big ears or deep voice, you can credit it to genes. But remember, not everyone will have the same family look, because your uncle may be part of your family by marriage, not by blood, because he married your mother's sister. His genes come from a totally different family.

WHY STUDY GENEALOGY?

Study genealogy and you will probably find yourself traveling to other times and other lands. You might discover that an ancestor on your father's side was a famous admiral. Maybe someone on your mother's side was a photographer who traveled all over the world! Discovering the occupations and abilities your ancestors had can open up whole new worlds for you. The more you know about your family and your past, the more you might discover about yourself. If a great-aunt was an important political speaker, maybe the power to lead is in your blood, too, and you can achieve much more than you ever thought you could! If a great-great-grandfather was a celebrated opera singer, maybe you should reconsider your shyness about joining the school chorus or try a capella singing!

Genealogy can help you discover your family's place in the world. And yours.

Getting Started

YOUR FAMILY HISTORY

Did you ever hear someone say, "I know you like a book?" Well, imagine that your family history is a book. It's the story of how you got where you are, filled with photographs and stories of long-ago family members growing up, and maps of where they lived. It begins way back when, with your earliest ancestor, and continues all the way down to you! Having a family scrapbook is a great way to know and understand your family. And knowing your family history is to really know yourself.

This book is going to show you how to learn about your own family history—which will actually help you to know more about yourself. Maybe you got your love of reading from your great-great-grandmother. Or maybe you might want to learn to cook once you find out a great-uncle was a celebrated chef. You can use this book on your own, with friends, or even suggest it to your teacher as a resource for a really fun class project. But whatever you choose, imagine how much fun it would be to bring your findings to your very own family reunion! See chapter 15 for more information about how to set that reunion up.

Your family history scrapbook will come, in time. It could be something you design digitally—you can find lots of programs to help you make a book that you can keep online. Then you can send it to family members via email, share on social media, or even print it out. If you'd rather have a physical book you can page through, keep an eye out for a big scrapbook you could use. You'll want to set aside a page (or two or three) for each family member, starting with the oldest, say, your great-great-grandfather, and moving down to the youngest, which might be you. To fill up this "family story" book, you'll need to collect information on each person, including photographs and special keepsakes, which you can later paste into your family scrapbook. Imagine! Under a picture of your grandmother, for example, you might have information on when and where she was born, what school she went to, whom she married, her likes and dislikes, and her famous apple pie recipe. Try to include other family "treasures," too, things that will remind you of her, such as a copy of her favorite joke, a report card, or a square cut from a dress she had when she was your age. All of these things, pasted into your scrapbook, will someday create a wonderful memory book to keep and display!

But before you can work on putting together your family scrapbook, you have to start gathering information—and have a place to put it!

STARTING OFF RIGHT

To start your genealogy research, you will need the right tools. You may want to set up all the files you need on your computer, or you may want to use a notebook. You'll definitely need a computer for your research, because it's a treasure trove of old photos and information.

You'll need a few supplies right away:

* A computer, tablet, or phone (if you have one).
* Some small notebooks—you should carry one with you at all times to make notes whenever you run across some great information.
* Sharpened pencils—be sure to keep a couple handy.
* A loose-leaf binder and paper, if you're doing things by hand.

When you get information on someone, put his or her name at the top of a page. Add the information to the page, and keep the page on your computer or in the binder. Each time you get new information, add it to the right person's page. Soon this document or binder will be your best friend: a genealogy workbook that will help you keep track of your family tree.

THOSE FAMILY PHOTOS

Once you show an interest in genealogy, you can be sure that someone is going to drag out an old dusty album of photographs. Actually, putting names and then facts and stories to the faces you see is a good part of the fun. Soon, you'll feel you really know them: the girl on the old merry-go-round, the serious young man in the sailor hat, the father proudly showing off the family car (with running boards).

Then there are those baby pictures, confirmation or bar mitzvah photos, and school and graduation pictures, too. You're sure to find yourself in there somewhere. The pictures in the album may not mean much to you now, but they will.

The important thing, right at the start, is to take good care of any photographs you want to look at or borrow to copy for your genealogy projects. Try not to touch the picture part itself, only the edges. Depending on the age and kind of paper the pictures are printed on, even oil from your fingers could damage them. Most of the older photographs that you will find in family albums will be the only copy anyone has. If they are damaged or lost, they can't be replaced, so you'll need to make copies if you want to cut, pin up, or glue any pictures. And if you borrow any, be sure to return them in the same condition that you got them in. You can easily scan photos into your computer, but make sure you handle them with the tender loving care they deserve. You don't want any tears or rips, and you certainly don't want fingerprints on such valuable items. You don't want to have a family feud on your hands!

A tintype from the 1890s

A common stereoscope

FUN FACTS

* Tintypes, the first "instant" photographs, were inexpensive and unbreakable. They were made out of metal!

* Stereoscopic pictures were two photos of the same thing placed side by side. With a stereoscopic viewer, you saw the picture in 3-D!

Your Family Tree

A family tree, as we said, isn't a tree but a kind of map. Instead of showing miles, a family tree shows how family members are related to one another. It can go back over many years; from you to your great-grandparents and beyond. The family tree form is called that because of the way it shows family members "branching out" from one another, like tree branches are connected to one another and to the trunk of the tree.

MAPPING YOUR FAMILY

Are you ready to begin drawing your family tree? Do you have enough information to begin? Yes, at least to start. You know who you are, and how you are related to your parents (you are their child). And you know how you are related to your grandparents, your parents' parents. So, let's start you off with a really simple family tree.

1. Find a large piece of paper, and make a circle near the bottom. On the inside, write your full name (first, middle, and last). Under your name, put your birth date (month, day, and year).

2. Make two lines going upward and draw two more circles at the top, like balloons. In one, write in one parent's full name and birth date. Write your other parent's full name and birth date in the other. (Ask for the correct spelling and birth dates.)

3. Make more lines going upward (more balloons): two from one parent's circle and two from the other parent's circle. Top each of them with two more circles. In these circles, write in your grandparents' full names—one parent's mother and father above one circle and one parent's mother and father above the other circle. Put in their birth dates.

That's a good start. Next, if you have brothers and sisters, and aunts and uncles, and cousins, you'll want to add them to your family tree, too. Your brothers and sisters are your siblings, which means that they are your parents' children, too. And your cousins are the children of your aunts and uncles. So they'll be listed on the family tree under their parents. This means you'll need a much bigger piece of paper, or some type of pedigree or genealogy form, to keep track of everybody! A genealogy program or app could also be a smart way to map out your tree.

FAMILY TREE TIPS

List each person in your family tree, then try to find out:

* ✳ when the person was born. Where.
* ✳ what schools the person went to. Years graduated.
* ✳ where the person lived.
* ✳ what jobs the person held.
* ✳ if a person was in the military. What service, where and when.
* ✳ if a person emigrated. From where and when.
* ✳ if the person is dead. When. Where. How. Where buried.

How much of this or other information you will want to put into your family tree diagram is up to you. But don't miss out on gathering the information while you can, so you can record it in your loose-leaf binder and later in your family scrapbook.

GROWING YOUR FAMILY TREE

Even if you start small, remember that big family trees grow from tiny roots. Here is a part of a family tree form. At the top would be the oldest relatives that you know, probably your grandparents. Vertical and horizontal lines map out your parents and their siblings, and you and your siblings, if you have them. Remember, you have two sets of grandparents—your mother's parents and your father's parents. That means you'll have eight great-grandparents. Your family tree will grow quickly once you start, so every time you learn about a relative, add his or her name to your family tree form, along with important vital statistics such as birth, marriage, and death dates. When you hear or find new stories about a relative, write them all down in your loose-leaf notebook. By the time you're finished, you should have a huge family tree that you can frame and hang in your room and a notebook filled with lots of family facts.

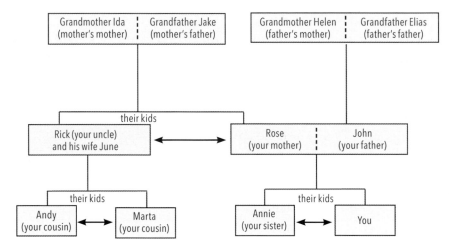

From this diagram it's easy to see how people in your family are related. Horizontal boxes side by side mean the people are siblings (brothers and sisters). Vertical lines tell us descent (who is the parent and who is the child). You can also see that your maternal grandmother and grandfather were married and had two kids.

With this kind of system, you can easily add more information. For example: Next to or beneath each name, you might write B (for birth) and D (for death) and put in the dates—at least the year, although the place is important, too. If the person is still living, put a small dash after the birth date. For example, if your birth year is 2007, you would write B2007–. Later on, after you've done some detective work, you'll have a lot more information to add.

If you want more information, write in M (for married) and the date. How would you show if someone was divorced? Since "D" stands for death, you can put a slash through the M and add the divorce date for M̶ 1982–1991.

BRINGING YOUR FAMILY TO LIFE

As you learn more about your family, you'll find yourself really getting to know them. You'll want to write down where family members were born, and when and where they got married (if they did). You will definitely want to add when, where, and how people died (if they are no longer living), and where they are buried. People often make visits to the graves of family members on departed relatives' birthdays or the anniversaries of their deaths. This is a good time for you to go, too. The person's full name and birth and death dates are etched on the cemetery gravestones. Be sure to bring one of your small notebooks and a pencil or two and take down the information, or simply take a picture of the tombstone with your phone. You may need it if you ever need to order a death certificate or find an obituary.

Death certificates are official papers issued at the time of death. If your family doesn't have a death certificate for a deceased grandparent, you should be able to order a copy for a fee from the local courthouse where the person lived, or from the Office or Bureau of Vital Statistics. You'll need the full name and year and place of death, and a reason for requesting the certificate.

Obituaries are much easier to find and often provide much more information. An obituary is a short biography of a person who died. Local newspapers print obituaries to tell their readers (often friends and neighbors of the deceased) that the person has passed away. Newspapers keep archives of everything they print. If you know the date a person died, you can search the archives of the local newspaper for that person's obituary, either online or in print. It is usually printed in an issue a day or two later. Libraries sometimes keep microfilm archives of old issues of local papers. An obituary can provide a lot of helpful information when you are researching your family tree.

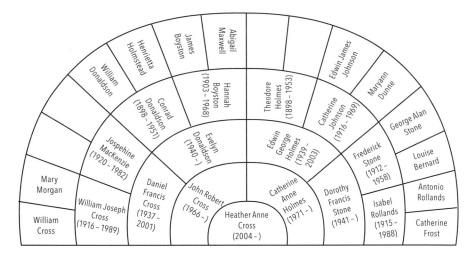

A fan-shaped pedigree chart such as this one is a good way to keep track of, and display, just your direct-line ancestors, rather than all family members. It is easy to see how several generations all come down to you.

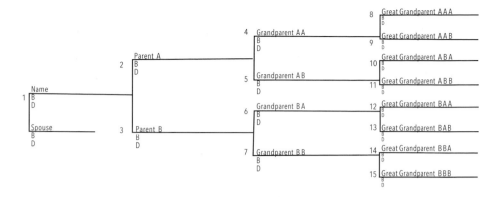

This type of pedigree form gives you room under the name line for important family details: date and place of birth, death, marriage; where buried, children's names, and other useful information you choose to include. Here, we include birth and death dates.

It can be extended as far back in time as you have room on the paper. If each ancestor on the chart is numbered, it is easy to key file folders to the chart, then arrange the folders accordingly.

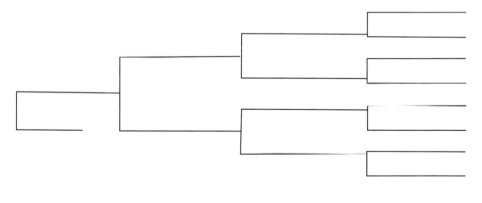

Key
Born
Died

4

Digging for Your Roots

Before you get to know your ancestors, let's start with the person and the people you know best—you and your immediate family! The answers you find here will start you on your genealogical trail.

HOW TO DO RESEARCH

Finding out facts about your family involves research. The first and easiest way to get some answers is simply by asking yourself some questions, or by interviewing your parents. This is called using primary sources, primary meaning "first." These are the people in your immediate family: your parents, yourself and your siblings. Start by finding out the basic facts—names, dates, places. Later on, when you've figured out who everybody is, you can go back to people and collect family stories, called recording "oral history." In the meantime, if you do need to get some quieter relatives talking, asking a few of the questions on pages 84–85 (taking oral histories) might help to draw them out.

START WITH WHAT YOU KNOW

You may be surprised to discover just how much important information about yourself you already know, and how much you need to find out. You probably know where you were born. But maybe you don't know the exact time of your birth—a fun thing to know. So ask your parents to help you make a copy of your birth certificate. Certificates are official records used in keeping track of what happens in people's lives. There are certificates for birth, baptism, marriage, and death. Each of these certificates can offer a wealth of information about you, and about the people in your family tree.

WATCH FOR TREASURE

As you research and do your interviews, keep an eye and ear out for these great sources of information:

1. Marriage license—where and when a family member was married.

2. Diploma—where and when someone went to school and earned a degree.

3. Death certificate or newspaper obituary notice—where and when someone died (sometimes how or why they died). Also, where they are buried, and what family members survived them.

4. Family Bible—births, marriages, and deaths may be recorded and the Bible handed down from generation to generation. A wonderful family heirloom.

5. Personal diaries and letters—names of family and friends (who could have important information), places the family might have lived (look at return addresses on envelopes), important details of daily lives and wonderful stories of the times in which the people lived.

6. Internet—all manner of information.

BEGIN AT THE BEGINNING

Birth records generally include the name of the child and the parents, and the exact date and even time of birth. The name of the hospital is there, too, and the signature of the doctor in charge. You might find some funny things, too, such as a footprint taken right after the baby was born, or a few strands of hair stuck to it.

Look at your birth certificate and you may notice that the name you've always used isn't exactly the one you were given at birth. If people call you Harry, your birth name may actually be Henry or Harold. Peggy is a common nickname for Margaret, but Peggy could actually be the name given on the birth certificate, not Margaret. Someone called Max might have been named Maximilian, after a long-ago Roman emperor, or Maxine!

As you search out old birth certificates, you might be surprised to find a person's last name isn't the same as on their birth certificate. It could be a simple spelling mistake, or that the person disliked the name and changed it. Sometimes, a name was simplified or changed when an immigrant moved to a new country with a different language and culture For example, Sandlovitz might have been shortened to Sands, while Roi (in French) was translated to King.

Time out for a holiday photo with visiting cousins.

LET'S TALK

Now that you've found out some basic family facts, you're ready to learn about interviewing. But asking questions, even of people you know well, isn't always easy. You'll need to know what questions to ask and how to ask them to get the answers you will find the most useful. Where do you start?

Think. Now that you have some information on family members, who do you think might be the most helpful? How about some of the oldest? Do you have several relatives who are about the same age, in their 60s or 70s, or maybe older?

Lucky you! These are the family members you want to talk to and interview, because they could be a great help to you in your genealogy research. Their stories of who their parents and grandparents were, where they came from, and how things were when they were kids are waiting to be told.

But people are different. Some are willing to talk about just anything for hours, while others need to be put at ease before they will open up to you. During an interview, one person will answer questions with only a word or two, so you'll need to ask follow-up questions to get the information you're looking for. Another person will ramble on with a long involved story instead of telling you what you want to know. You need to take control of the interview and bring the talkative ones back on track.

It's nice to have the family dog in the picture.

SETTING UP AN INTERVIEW

To get ready to interview, before you sit down to ask questions, you'll need some way to catch and keep the responses people give you, and whatever else they may say. A good way is to use a tape recorder or a cell phone, if you have one, and don't forget to use fresh batteries and keep your phone charged. That way, you'll have a record of any valuable information and be able to listen to it again and again to refresh your memory. After the interview, you'll want to transcribe, or copy, the words onto paper or type them up to have easy access to it. If someone objects or is clearly uncomfortable being recorded, go back to that old standby of information-gathering—a notebook and a few pencils or pens.

ASKING QUESTIONS!

To make your research easier (and for organizing the information in your workbook later on), it helps to have a form that can be filled out. That way, you can be sure to ask the same basic questions of everyone you interview. For relatives you can't talk to in person because they don't live nearby, you can send the form in an email. For your relatives who like snail mail better, put your questionnaire in an envelope and send it along with a self-addressed stamped envelope so they can get it back to you quickly and easily. Explain what the genealogy project you're doing is and that you'd like each family member to fill out the form for you. Politely request that they send back the completed form by a certain date (allowing two weeks or so is about right). That way the form is less likely to be put aside and forgotten or mislaid.

Copy this form, or make up one of your own:

1. Full name (first, middle, last)
2. Date and place of birth
3. Parent A's name
4. Parent B's name
5. Current address
6. Previous addresses (years, when moved)
7. Education (when, where)
8. Health concerns
9. Employment history

10. Married (name of spouse, date, location; include multiple lines for multiple marriages)

11. Children (names, dates, places of birth)

12. Divorced date, place; include multiple lines here, too)

13. Military service (date of service, branch)

14. Awards and honors received

15. Memberships (club, church, organization)

16. Pets

17. Special talents

Is there anything else about yourself that you would like me to know?

Who else should receive a copy of this form (name, relationship, address)?

Asking these last questions might get you some information you wouldn't have thought to ask about and could lead to family members you don't know. As you discover relatives you didn't know, add their names to your list of people to be interviewed or sent a copy of the form.

It's a good idea, too, to leave space at the bottom of your form for any "Comments" or "Stories." If the form appears to have very little blank space, indicate to your relatives that they can add any additional information they would like on the back of the form or on a separate sheet of paper. Note: Remember to ask each relative to email or send a nice close-up photo (a head shot) that you can keep.

How far back can you go?

It's thrilling to have all that information coming in! As the forms are filled out or returned, use a three-hole punch along the left side and put the pages into your loose-leaf binder. Or scan them into files on your computer. Add only basic facts (such as birth date) to your working family tree. Later, you'll use a lot more of this helpful and interesting information in making up your family history scrapbook. For now, keep the forms all neat and safe in one handy place, your loose-leaf genealogy workbook or in neatly organized files on your computer.

BE PREPARED!

Even when you're not planning to interview anyone, keep your phone or a small notebook and a couple of sharp pencils or pens with you at all times. You never know when you might need them! At a family dinner, your father might start talking about the time his uncle won first prize in a yodeling contest. Or you could be driving home with your mother when she starts telling you about how her grandfather won a lot of money in a lottery. Remember, when you record the information, write down who told you it and where and when you got the information. Later, if you need to, you can go back to that person ("primary source") and ask for more information about a particular ancestor. Like the detectives on TV cop shows, whip out your notebook and jot things down. You can refer to them later, to jog your memory or your source's.

SPEAKING THE LINGO

Genealogy work has its own language. Here's a list of vocabulary words that should help you in researching your family history:

Ancestor—your ancestors are the people you are descended from—your parents' parents, their parents, and so on.

Archives—a collection of historical records and items: birth and death records, land deeds; back issues of old newspapers.

Autobiography—a life story, told by the person writing or speaking it.

Biography—a life story, told by someone else.

Census—an official count of residents (who they are, where they live) taken at certain times, such as every ten years.

Descendant—someone younger than you in your family lineage—your children, and their children; someone you are an ancestor of.

Emigrate—to move from one country to another to start a new life elsewhere.

Fraternal twins—siblings born at the same time, but not from the same egg. (Compare to Identical twins.)

Genealogy—a "mapping" of family members, from the farthest-back ancestor to the living members of the family.

Generation—family members on the same "step" of family history (great-grandparents, grandparents, parents).

Genes—biologically, what makes you who you are (DNA code).

Head(s) of household—the adult(s) responsible for a family group.

Identical twins—siblings born at the same time from the same egg. (Compare to Fraternal twins.)

Immigrant—a person who enters a country to stay and live permanently.

Maiden name—Surname of an unmarried woman, which may change at marriage.

Maternal—"from the mother." Relatives on your maternal side are directly related to your mother.

Paternal—"from the father." Relatives on your paternal side are directly related to your father.

Pedigree—a person's record, in chart form, of parental and ancestral information (similar in meaning to genealogy).

Relatives—people related to you.

Sibling—brother or sister.

Spouse—husband or wife.

Surname—a person's last or "family" name.

5

Getting Organized

In the digital age, you can easily make and keep track of many, many folders on your computer and have them all at your fingertips. Start with one folder named MY FAMILY TREE. Within that folder, you can make up other folders, one for each family member. Be sure to label each folder with the person's name. Inside those folders, you can store photos, records, copies of important documents, and even favorite recipes or hobbies of your ancestors.

Many free genealogy programs are available online to help you create your family tree and make it bloom. Take a look at trees.ancestory.com or familyecho.com, smilebox.com or freedigitalscrapbooking.com. You can choose from many layout styles and customize every page just the way you want, with illustrations or photos. And best of all, when you're done, you can email your digital scrapbook, print it out, or even put it on Facebook.

If you prefer, you can also organize things the old school way—the way your ancestors might have done! Remember the loose-leaf binder we suggested you might want to get? You'll definitely want to have one specific place to keep it and all that family information you've been gathering. A big binder that you keep at home (you won't want to be carrying it around with you) is something you'll always be able to find. It will be your genealogical workbook and hold tons of detailed information. Your family tree diagram just maps out your family relationships, but the information stored in your loose-leaf binder can be used to put together a family scrapbook, along with pictures, quotations from letters, and other interesting things you've discovered about family members.

YOUR GENEALOGICAL WORKBOOK

You can organize your genealogical workbook in different ways on your computer. The easiest way is to give your family members their own digital folders or pages. Put the name of each family member at the top of a separate page. You probably know more about yourself than about any of your family members. So, start with your name and set up the page in the binder so that when you open it, your page is on top. Next, put in a page for each of your siblings (sisters and brothers), if any, then your parents and their siblings—your aunts and uncles. (You will probably need to interview each of them to get information to fill in the pages.) After the pages for your aunts and uncles will be your grandparents' pages, with their names at the top, and so on. This way, you can go back in time, from generation to generation, as far as your genealogical research takes you.

You'll soon see, as you gather information and talk to and find out more about your relatives, that the information in your folder will grow and grow.

More organizing tips

Your computer or your loose-leaf binder is your best friend. It's here where you'll rewrite neatly your scribbled interview notes or copy down your taped interviews. Be sure to write down the date of the interview and the name of the person interviewed. You may have more questions to ask or need to update your notes.

A blackboard with chalk, whiteboard with erasable marker or, better yet, a cork bulletin board, index cards, and pushpins come in handy, too. You can post things to be done—such as family members to follow up with, as you do your research. Most computers also have "sticky note" features and reminders to help you stay right on track.

The key here is to be sure to label everything!

Special occasion photos, like fiftieth wedding anniversaries, can help to fix the date of the picture.

Good ways to keep "keepsakes"

As you grow your family tree, you're going to run across items you'll want to keep. They won't fit in your binder and may even be too bulky for your scrapbook. Photo boxes or plain old shoeboxes make great catchalls. They're perfect for envelopes of photos (remember to identify who's in the pictures), folded or rolled copies of birth certificates and other documents and vital records, expired passports, and drivers' licenses. Letters from a homesick soldier, a child away at camp for the first time, or a stack of old love letters are wonderful family keepsakes. You'll want to hold onto military awards and medals, of course, but old school report cards are also fun to have. Note: If you need two or more boxes to hold everything, separate the contents and label or code the containers to make finding things easier.

If you want to, you can also scan the documents and take digital photographs of the items you have and then upload them onto your computer. Whatever method works best for you is the right way to do it.

Keep things together

If paperwork and other keepsakes are piling up, designate a section of your room as your genealogical research center. You might even want to put up a sign that says so. Keep any notebooks you've been using here. Store your oversize or treasured photographs in sturdy flat boxes that will keep them safe, and keep odd-size items neatly in photo albums or shoeboxes. Your loose-leaf binder (or binders if you are using more than one), should be where they are easy to reach and

work with. And don't forget—every time you gather a new piece of information, be sure to bring it right to this special area. A bulletin board is a good idea, so that small scribbled notes can be posted and won't get lost. It's a reminder, too, to follow-up or transfer the information into your binder later on or scan into your computer. Don't put it off too long, because that's how valuable information can get lost—and how a neat and tidy area can quickly morph into a messy one.

"MY FAMILY" BOX

Why not consider a file box with separators and manila folders, to keep things in place? (You'll want to decorate it, of course.)

WHAT YOU NEED

* box about 12" x 12" x 9" deep
* cardboard
* markers
* stick-on labels
* glue
* copies of photos, clippings, to decorate box
* scissors
* shellac
* small brush
* manila folders (with tabs)

WHAT TO DO

1. Cut cardboard to fit box (12" x 9 1/2"), and use as separators.

2. Print labels, or use markers to write them: Maternal Side, Paternal Side, Maternal Grandparents, Paternal Grandparents, etc.

3. Attach labels to the sides of the separators. Change the positions of each label so each heading will be visible!

4. Cut around the copies of family photos (remember, these are copies, not priceless originals, but double-check anyway before cutting, gluing, or shellacking anything!). Be sure to include pictures from both sides of your family. Dot-glue the back of the photographs and paste them all over the box.

5. Dip your brush into the shellac and carefully paint over your photos and the box. This will give it a protective covering and a nice shine.

6. On manila folders, use a marker that makes the words really stand out. Write the person's name, and put papers relating to that person in the folder. If you have too many, put the person's name on the folder, and then add "birth certificate," "diary pages," or "army records" to additional manila folders.

Label, label, label

You might want to invest in some labels to stick on the back of photographs. Regular labels are made to stay on, which is fine if the photographs are your own. If photographs are borrowed, use removable labels to identify them, so you can return them in the same condition you received them. On the label, clearly identify the date, place, and person or persons in the photo (reading from left to right). Tip: Do this while looking at the photo, and place the label on after you write it all out. You are less likely to make a mistake in writing down the information, and there is less danger of damaging the photo from pressing too hard or having ink bleed through to the photograph. Be sure the ink is dry before "stacking" photos. When you scan these valuable photos, don't forget to scan the back, too, so you have all the information on the label, as well as whatever name you're giving the photo when you save it on your computer.

While we are talking about labels, don't forget to save the interviews you do on your phone with recognizable file names, so you'll be able to find them when you upload them onto your computer.

Caring for photographs

There are photographs and there are photographs. If you've just handed out a dozen copies of your latest class picture to relatives, it's no big deal if one or two become misplaced or lost or accidentally damaged. But if your great aunt lets you borrow the only picture of her mother taken when she was a schoolgirl, so that you can make a copy, it's a different story. Lose it, and it's gone! Sticky fingerprints, ink from markers, spills, or creases from handling a photo carelessly can destroy a cherished keepsake.

Turning sixteen has always been a reason to have a portrait taken.

PHOTO HANDLING TIPS

✳ Hold all photos by the edges. Try not to touch the picture itself.

✳ Put photographs in clean envelopes or inside a folded sheet of acid-free paper to protect them.

✳ When mailing or carrying photographs, add a stiff piece of cardboard backing to keep the photograph flat (older photographs can be especially fragile and easily creased).

✳ Be careful writing on the backs of photographs. Marker ink can soak into older paper, and writing with pen or pencil can make impressions that show through on the picture side (write on regular or removable labels and attach them instead).

✳ Don't use tape on the front (picture side) of the photographs (if necessary, for example, to stop a tear from causing more damage, attach tape to the back).

✳ Definitely don't cut up any one-of-a-kind photographs or use them in any projects. Make copies! The best idea is to scan them and upload to your computer so you will always have them safe at hand. Then, you won't have to worry about damage.

Finding your place

Papers and notepads and books—oh, my! At some point a bookmark—or several—might come in handy. Of course, you can use just about anything for a bookmark, but why not make special bookmarks, starring family members, for a cool way to mark your place in your genealogy research.

Where should you start? How about with you? Are you the baby of the family? The big sister? The pesky little brother? We all have roles to play, based on birth order and our position in the family (and many of us play those roles to the hilt). Show your place in the family. Search out a good photo of yourself and clip out of magazines some small pictures that say, "This is me!" If you're nuts about sports, decorate your bookmark with pictures of sports equipment, for example, pictures of soccer, baseball, football, or tennis balls, or of players in action. You're the "princess" of the family? Cut out a crown, or draw one, for your head. Some pasted-on "jewels" will also show your regal side. Small squares cut from blue jeans (if you're the rough-and-tumble sort) or bits of lace (for the more ladylike), it's up to you.

Birthdays are happy occasions for keepsake photos.

A tintype photo keeps family very near throughout the years.

FAMILY BOOKMARKS

This easy, creative activity is designed to help you get to know your family members better and keep you organized, too. And, of course, family bookmarks make great "thank you" gifts to send to those special people in your family who helped with your research.

WHAT YOU NEED:

✳ poster board

✳ scissors

✳ photos, clippings, scraps, or small mementos

✳ glue

✳ markers

WHAT TO DO:

1. Cut the poster board to a good bookmark size, say 2" wide x 8" long.

2. Arrange the photo (or photos) with whatever else you choose on the bookmark. Adjust the positions until you are happy with the appearance.

3. Glue each piece to the bookmark. Once the front side is dry, you can use the markers to decorate the back if you wish—or glue or tape a long piece of colorful ribbon or yarn to it.

Now make some bookmarks showing other family members. The more the merrier!

6

Searching Online

Suppose you've gathered information about your immediate family by asking your parents questions about yourself and your family. You've started a family tree and filled out some forms. You've labeled interview recordings and have typed up the interview text and saved it on your computer or in your binder. You and your parents have searched through family papers and records.

Now you need to dig deeper and farther back in time. A lot of the information you're looking for won't be things you know, or even things your parents know. Where do you go from here? The answer could be as near as your computer or as far as your local library.

Just as your parents and relatives are your primary sources of genealogy information, the public records you can search are your secondary sources. They will help you dig deeper, and go farther and farther back into time.

When it comes to those secondary sources for researching your family tree, your computer is a great help. Online, you can find information, listings, even copies of documents, but you have to know how to search, what to look for, and where to look.

You probably have a favorite Internet search engine already. Google and Yahoo are two popular search engines you can use in your online journey to find information about your family!

STARTING THE "SEARCH"

Here's an example: Let's say your grandfather told you that his grandfather came to the United States in the early 1900s. You don't know the year, and you don't know how he traveled. First, you would go to your favorite search engine and type in his name. Put quotation marks around the name so the search engine will search for the first and last names together. Did you get any hits? Maybe not, or maybe you are surprised to see a list of several people with that name. Can you narrow the search? Check the details given: the year, the age of the person, where he emigrated from or where he lived. If the names listed are clearly not your grandfather's grandfather, don't give up. Other search engines could have access to different information, and there are other places to search.

FINDING VITAL RECORDS

Do you have any idea where your great-great-grandfather lived and worked, and when and where did he die? For that sort of information, your next stop would be to search websites that provide free access to vital records (many websites charge a fee for use, but allow you to try it out first free). Vital records are official records of birth, death, marriage, and divorce organized by state or county in the United States. Some of this information is also picked up by genealogical sites, such as familysearch.com, or ancestry.com. At the site, you type in your relative's name and any other details that might be helpful. But have patience. Searches can take time, especially if you have to check different states or locate appropriate websites in different countries.

As you do your searches, you may come up with many bits of information about your relative. You may find his social security number (available online after a person has passed away), his wife's name, where they were married, where they lived, and even his occupation—all terrifically helpful. Save the information in your digital files, print it out for your binder, or write the results of your searches onto that relative's loose-leaf page, date it, and copy down the full web address at the top.

CHECKING CENSUS RECORDS

Census records are another "must" search for information on ancestors who lived in the United States at least seventy year ago. A census is a count of people who live in an area. These records are taken at certain times, generally every ten years, in countries around the world. Census takers go from door to door and fill out forms on every person living at that address. Sometimes, people are asked to fill out and send back census forms that they receive in the mail. So, if you search for your great-great-grandfather's

name in the census records and find it, you'll learn a lot of things about him and about other family members living at that time at the same address. Go to earlier and later census records and you will be able to track changes in the family from census to census, such as new

births (age 7 in 1830), and likely deaths (was 82 in 1830; in 1840 no longer living at that address), job changes, and much more.

In the U.S., census records are available for every decade from 1790 to 1940. To protect the privacy of the people who responded, census records are not available until seventy-two years after the census was taken. Before that, records can only be obtained by the person whose name is in the census. You won't be able to see the 1950 census until April 1, 2022. Information from some census records may be found online. To actually see and examine a particular filled-out census form, you may need to go to a federal archive facility.

Offices in various parts of the country make these records available for genealogy research and other purposes. You can also find free census records at places like https://www .censusrecords.com or https://familysearch.org.

Information available on census forms:

* Address or name of house
* Given name and surname of each person at the address
* Relationship to head of household
* Marital status

* Age at last birthday
* Profession or occupation
* Employment status
* Birthplace

LINKING UP

As you do your online research, you'll often find links to other websites where you might find more information to speed you along in your search. If you're lucky enough to find yourself at a website with a whole lot of information about your family, don't lose it! Enter it as a favorite so your browser will make it available to you whenever you want to go back to it. It might be a good idea, too, to keep track of all the websites you're using in a separate document.

CHECKING GOOGLE IMAGES

Google Images (https://images.google.com) is a great place to search for photos of your ancestors or find photos from the time periods when they lived. Make sure that the images are listed as free. Then you will know that it's okay to use them. Otherwise, you need to pay, and that might be beyond your budget.

USING SOCIAL MEDIA

You'd be amazed at the information you can find on Facebook, Twitter, or Instagram. Long-lost friends often regain contact there, and that means long-lost relatives, too. If you don't have a Facebook page, you might want to ask your parents if it's all right for you to put one up. You could call it something like "Looking for Vazquez Ancestors." That way, people can find you, too. You can also search Facebook and Twitter for people who share your last name and see if you are related or if they have information you might be able to use. But—and this is crucially important—be sure to read the social media safety tips sidebar on page 50.

The basics of searching

In case doing searches online is new to you, here are a few tips about how to go about it:

1. Connect search words in quotes; for example, "Clutters Boston" for a Clutter family who lived in Boston. The search engine will look for both "Clutters" and "Boston" together. That way you will avoid getting search results about closet clutters or the Boston Red Sox.

2. Don't bother with small, connecting words like "the," "and," and "or." Search engines ignore them.

3. Be specific if you know details: your great-uncle was a member of "Knights of Columbus Baltimore 1900s." If you're not sure, search instead for "Men's Organizations Maryland 1900s" and check out the hits that come up.

Some Internet files can be very long, and would waste a lot of paper and ink if you printed them. If possible, copy and paste the information you want to keep to a file and save it that way. Otherwise, remember to carefully record all the information you find in your digital genealogy folder for safekeeping. Make a note of the website where you got the information, so you can return to it if you need to.

SOCIAL MEDIA SAFETY

Social media is wonderful, but you need to be careful. Sometimes people masquerade as other people. Someone whose picture suggests they are 15 years old might actually be 45 years old! Other times, people like to play pranks or get you to click on a link so they can collect data on you or even infect your computer with a virus.

Follow these tips to stay safe online!

* Make sure your parents know that you are going onto social media. You might want to have them present when you do.

* Never give out your home address, email address, age, or phone number.

* Don't put personal photos up on your social media account, because your search is going to be public.

* Make sure that if anyone responds, you check with your parents before going ahead with your research.

* Don't download anything from people you do not know.

* Don't accept friend requests from anyone who is not your friend in real life. If that person seems like a relative, get your parents involved to see if it is safe for you to connect with that person.

PAY-FOR-INFORMATION SITES

In doing only a few searches, you will notice that some genealogical sites ask you to "sign in" and some have fees for using the site. Should you pay for access to information? That depends on how far you have gotten with your searches, and how important it is for you to have access to information that you can't seem to find elsewhere. Check with your parents. They might have other leads to help you find what you are looking for.

If you are just starting out, it is much more fun to see just how far you can get on your own. Later, if and when you've hit a dead end, or there are "holes" in your research that you're trying to fill, paying a small fee might be worth it. If you and your parents decide it's a reasonable expense, test out a likely website if you can before signing up for the paid service. Some sites will let you do a few searches at no charge to give you an idea of the kind of information and how much is available. Maybe a few minutes' work will fill that "hole" in your research without the need to plunk down a good part of your allowance or hard-earned cash.

Photos from those far away remind you to keep in touch.

Showing off new spring outfits is a time-honored tradition.

7

Tracking Your Ancestors

WHERE ARE YOUR ANCESTORS FROM?

Part of what makes genealogy so fascinating is that you aren't just tracing your family back through time, but through place as well. You may live in America now, but only Native Americans are original natives. Everyone else came from someplace else. That could mean that you have cousins in Ireland, China, South Africa, Peru, or somewhere else in the world. On the other hand, if you live in those countries now, your family may have moved there from a different country a long time ago. Records, if they still exist, could be hard to find or written in a different language. No matter where you are, chances are that some family members immigrated to the U.S. in the past. So whether you have lost touch with your American cousins, or want to trace your family back to the "old country," here's one place to try.

COMING TO AMERICA

Go to a computer and type in the search phrase "Ellis Island." From 1892 to 1954, millions of people passed through the Ellis Island Immigration Center on their way to new lives in the U.S. They sailed on ships into New York harbor from many different countries. Each person arriving on Ellis Island was given certain tests. The immigrants were examined by a doctor and given simple wooden puzzles to test their skill and intelligence. Imagine how difficult it was for people who didn't speak the language to figure out what they were expected to do with these pieces of wood. But the immigrants came because once inside the U.S., a whole new life awaited them.

Today, people come from everywhere to visit Ellis Island and touch the names of ancestors etched into its "Wall of Honor." The Ellis Island website, ellisisland.org, can also help people find names on passenger lists. If your great-great-great grandfather didn't come through Ellis Island, do other searches under "immigration" (another incoming center was Angel Island in San Francisco Bay) and you just might be able to tell your grandfather something he doesn't know about his grandfather.

Were your relatives among them? How would you go about finding out? First, of course, ask your parents or older relatives. Maybe someone in your family has an old passport or some immigration papers from another country. A passport is a document that allows people to travel from country to country. Inside the passport booklet, look for visa stamps, those special dated markings that tell when a family member passed from one country to another. Passports usually have a photograph of the family member, too. If your family often travels together, one of your parents' passports might include you, too. Some of your relatives may have emigrated before passports were used. They might have been issued immigration or travel documents, and these papers will provide information that you can record in your loose-leaf workbook and onto your family tree.

THE U.S. BECAME THEIR HOME

✳ Knute Rockne, Notre Dame's famed football coach, arrived in the U.S. from Norway, in 1893.

✳ Frank Capra, director of the Christmas favorite, *It's a Wonderful Life*, emigrated from Italy in 1903.

✳ Entertainer Bob Hope came through Ellis Island in 1908 from England.

✳ Bela Lugosi, famous for playing Dracula, emigrated from Hungary in 1921.

✳ Science fiction writer Isaac Asimov came to the U.S. from Russia in 1923.

✳ The Von Trapp family, made famous by *The Sound of Music*, came to the U.S. from Austria in 1938.

If the document includes a photo of the traveler, you'll definitely want to copy it for that family scrapbook you are working on. Adding copies of interesting visa stamps will bring your ancestors' travels to life.

Easter bonnets are a reason to "smile for the camera."

WHAT'S IN A NAME?

Today more than 100 million Americans can claim an ancestor who arrived through Ellis Island. And millions of people throughout the world can claim ancestors who came to the U.S. and stayed! But finding them isn't always easy.

If you're looking for a relative with the last name Schmidt, for example, you may not find him. Why not? His real name might have been Schmitter or something similar. Names may have been spelled incorrectly, or intentionally changed. An immigration official may have made a mistake filling out a form or simply misunderstood what an immigrant said. Newcomers themselves also changed their names, wanting to fit in. They worried that employers and others would find their names hard to pronounce.

For that reason, many Asian immigrants even today take on new first names or nicknames, such as Tina or Harry, instead of using their birth names. Traditional Asian names are written with the surname first and the given name last: Ishikawa (last name) Akihiko (first name) instead of Akihiko Ishikawa. If Alexander Hamilton had been Asian, his name would have been written "Hamilton Alexander."

Or, if immigrants escaped from the country they left (for example, to avoid the draft), they might even have worried that if their real names were known, officials "back home" could find them and bring them back.

Other ethnic groups had their own naming traditions. In Swedish tradition, a girl named Christine whose father's name was Lars would be called Christine Larsdotter and her brother's last name would have been Larssen. The fact that family members had different last names was confusing to some people, so a new surname, like Olson, was selected.

Other immigrants Americanized their names: Finkelstein became Fink, the German name Schneider (meaning tailor) became Taylor, the Polish first name Wojciech changed to Albert, while the Russian Misha or Mikhail became Michael.

When doing searches, keep possible name changes, spellings, nicknames, and abbreviations in mind. Frederick might be listed as Friedrich, Fred, or Freddy; Richard as Ricardo or Rico; James might be given as Jamie or Jimmy, or abbreviated to Jas.

So, if searching for Mikhail Romanov doesn't work, for example, try Michael Romanov, Mike Romanov, or just M. Romanov. Some websites might offer alternate spellings of the name you entered, even for last names. For Romanov, you might find such alternates as Romanoff, Romanofsky/Romanofski, Romanovsky/Romanovski, Romanowsky/Romanowski, and even Romanovitz/Romanowitz. Be sure to give these a look, too. If you're unsure of the spelling of a name, take guesses and see if the information you need comes up. Remember, part of genealogy is having hunches, and thinking just like a detective!

A very long time ago, some people took their occupation as their surname. Henry Miller milled grains, while Tom Smith was a smithy, someone who shoed horses. If your name is Shepherd, it's possible that an ancestor may have herded sheep. Chances are your family isn't in that business anymore!

WHEN NAMES CHANGE

Many names have foreign origins. Michelle is a French name but, after crossing the ocean, it has stayed the same. Other names, however, have changed, and knowing this might help you find your ancestors a bit more easily. Here is a name game to give you some practice. See if you can match the list of the names on the left with their correct counterparts in the right-hand column. The answer is on page 58.

Pablo	Rebecca
Jacques	Anthony
Tamio	Beatrice
Maurice	Amy
Rivka	Paul
Aimee	Morris
Antonio	John
Bice	Thomas

FUN FACT

America has been called the "great melting pot." What does this mean? Think about what would happen if someone were to put crayons of all kinds together into a pot and heat it up. The wax would melt and the colors, shapes, and textures of all the crayons would blend together. So, calling America a melting pot means that all the aspects of the different cultures where people came from have created a new mixture that is truly American!

WHO YOU ARE IS A CLUE

Where to search on the Internet for genealogical information on your family tree depends on your ethnic background. Many African Americans today, for example, are descendants of enslaved people taken from their homes along the coastline between the Congo and Gambia Rivers in East Africa. Starting in 1619, these forced immigrants were uprooted, transported to the Americas and the Caribbean in ships, and sold as slaves. Most lost their proud African names to slave names, or took the plantation owner's last name as their own. That's why, in some small rural towns in the South, almost an entire population can have the same last name. But, no matter where your ancestors come from or who they were, there are archives available online to help you trace your ancestors back through several generations. One popular website, cyndislist.com, has links to a fascinating array of archives.

Answer key:

Pablo = Paul * Jacques = John * Tamio = Thomas * Maurice = Morris * Rivka = Rebecca * Aimee = Amy * Antonio = Anthony * Bice = Beatrice

FORGING CULTURAL LINKS ON THE GENEALOGY CHAIN

If you're looking for information on a missing family member, don't forget those important cultural ties. Just because people move to a new country doesn't mean they leave the old culture behind. They usually arrange to live near and get together often with people who speak the same language, eat the same foods, and enjoy the same things. Homesick for parts of the culture left behind, new immigrants stick together and try to re-create what is comfortable and familiar.

When large numbers of people were immigrating to the U.S, ethnic neighborhoods quickly sprang up—Chinatown, Germantown, Little Italy. This "coming together" of nationalities

was repeated in large cities all across the country. These cultural enclaves helped make America Home Sweet Home for a wonderfully diverse group of people.

What parts of your ancestors' culture is still a part of your life? Is it your great Chinese grandmother's cold noodles and sesame sauce? Your great-great Italian grandmother's lasagna? The Greek songs your aunt sings at family gatherings? The folk dances the men in your family perform at celebrations? The piñata you break open at parties? What things in your life today are pieces of your cultural history?

Just as your mother's blue eyes might have been handed down to you, so, too, have certain cultural traits. What did your great-grandmother teach your grandmother, who taught your mother, who taught you? As these things pass from one generation to the next, they often change to meet the needs of the times. Your grandmother might have taught your mother to make her special Russian pudding with cream, but when your mother taught you, she might have used milk instead—or added raisins. How will you pass this down or change it for your children? These family recipes are part of your cultural heritage and something you'll want to preserve in your special family history scrapbook. You can paste your grandmother's recipe for blueberry bread into her section, and your aunt's recipe for Mexican refried beans into hers.

Knowing about your ancestors' culture can help you find your ancestors, too. Look for leads to a Chinese ancestor in the Chinese community. If an Italian ancestor was famous for her pasta sauce, maybe an Italian community newspaper did a story about her. Local papers and community organizations of all nationalities are good sources of information. Maybe someone knew your grandmother when she lived in a different town. Or perhaps someone remembers the name of your grandmother's best friend. You

An old family photo might include your grandma, and her twin, as kids.

can find wonderful clues where you never even expected to.

All you have to do is ask your relatives or ask people at cultural events you attend with your family.

8

Heraldry

IT STARTED WITH THE KNIGHTS

If you've already tried to research your family name on the Internet, you might have found yourself at a website that talked about heraldry, and something called a coat of arms.

Coats of arms began about a thousand years ago (the twelfth century—that means the 1100s) in Europe. It was a time when knights wore full—and very heavy—suits of armor. At a distance, or with their head armor covering their faces, it was nearly impossible to identify friend from foe. During the noise of battle, knights couldn't speak loudly enough to be heard and recognized. A quick and visual way was needed to identify who was who.

So knights put identifying marks on their shields. They wore the same design on the loose cloth cape that covered their armor to protect them from the sun's heat. The markings on the "coat" of arms allowed a knight to be recognized, even if he was separated from his shield.

Gradually, people from noble or high-class families began to use coat of arms markings. The working poor often couldn't read or write, so these "picture names" helped them, too.

Soon the identifying marks became more complex. People added symbols of honors they had won or to commemorate important family events and special occasions. Having a coat of arms became a mark of great pride. And the status from the coat of arms was something the whole family, or clan, could share.

With so many new coats of arms being worn, and new ones being made up, a procedure was set up to register and keep track of the many symbols that appeared on them. Even today, who is entitled to wear what on a coat of arms is strictly regulated in some countries.

FUN FACTS

* Lucky you, if you were the oldest son in the Middle Ages. You inherited your father's coat of arms intact. A younger son would only have the right to place a smaller picture in the middle of a shield.

* If you were a woman getting married, you would bring your family's coat of arms into your husband's, adding to the design.

THE COAT OF ARMS

A coat of arms is made up of several different parts. The main sections are:

1. CREST—a small simple design that originally decorated a knight's helmet. The crest alone was never meant to represent family, but it's used today to personalize stationery or to stamp a special design into envelope sealing wax.

2. SHIELD—a half-oval shape. Early shields often held just a simple pattern; later ones were divided into quarters, showing designs representing the maternal and paternal family lines.

3. SUPPORTERS—a pair of animals or objects on either side of the shield. These family protectors were chosen for their strength, intelligence, or cunning. Lions, tigers, or bears were popular supporters.

4. MOTTO—a short phrase or saying. Some families today have silly mottoes like "When the going gets tough, the tough go shopping."

What would be your family motto?

TRACING YOUR COAT OF ARMS

Do you have a coat of arms? If so, your family name may not be enough to find it. Individuals, and not families, were awarded coats of arms. So, even if your family name is not as common as Smith, you may find a choice of coats of arms given for your name.

How do you tell which one might be your family coat of arms?

You would need to find out which coat of arms was granted to a particular ancestor. It may be possible to track a likely coat of arms based on where your ancestor lived. But that may not be easy. There could have been many people in that village with that same last name. And some coats of arm are listed only by country, rather than village.

If you really want to find out if an ancestor was ever awarded an actual coat of arms, search out and contact the College of Arms in your ancestor's country. You'll probably be asked for details on your genealogy and be charged a fee, but you may end up finding an official coat of arms connected to you through a family member.

SOMETHING ALL MY OWN

It wouldn't be official, but that's no reason why you couldn't make up a coat of arms of your own. What could you put on it? Just about anything. You might want to display your country's flag, and the national flags of your ancestors. You could show your ethnic pride by including a drawing of the Egyptian pyramids or the Great Wall of China, the "boot" shape of Italy, or a kangaroo. Even showing a food, such as two crossed crusty loaves of French bread, can represent your nationality. Family events can be drawn onto the shield: a knight with a sword, the landing of the *Mayflower*, the broken chains of slavery. You might choose to show the blue ribbon you won in a horse show, a skateboard because skateboarding is your favorite sport, a chess piece, musical notes or the instrument you play, or anything else that means something to you.

MY COAT OF ARMS

Have you ever heard the expression "come through with flying colors"? It means to hold a flag high in victory after a battle, clearly showing the winner's coat of arms. Luckily, you won't need to fight a battle. First, just create a coat of arms. Later you can make it larger, attach it to a stick, and proudly fly your own colors!

WHAT YOU NEED:

* tracing paper
* markers, pencils, and paints
* paper sheets
* scissors
* glue
* construction paper in different colors

WHAT TO DO:

1. Start with the shield. Trace one of the shapes given here, or draw one of your own, in the center of a sheet of paper. You can also enlarge it, or cut out a pattern, then cut a shield from heavy construction paper.

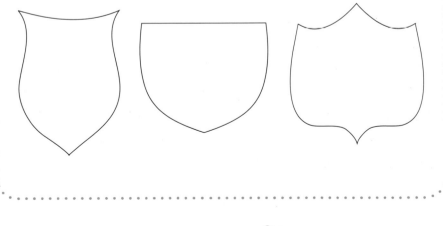

2. Draw lines to divide the shield in half or into quarters. Use glue and construction paper or markers to add stripes of your favorite colors. Draw small pictures on your shield.

3. Draw a crest above the shield—a small and easy-to-recognize drawing to represent you or your family.

4. If you wish, add a pair of supporters—one on each side of the shield, facing the center.

5. Think of a motto (short is best) and print it at the bottom of your coat of arms. It looks nicer on a ribbon, but you don't need one, just the motto.

Now you have a coat of arms. You can hang it on the outside of your door, or frame it and hang it up in your room.

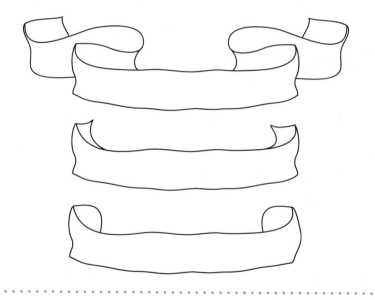

More information on heraldry and making your own coat of arms can be found at www.yourchildlearns.com/heraldry.htm.

9

Making the Connections

Imagine that some relatives you've never met have come to visit. Suddenly one of them steps up to you and shakes your hand. "Hi, I'm Fred Jacobs, your third cousin, twice removed."

"Huh?" You know what a cousin is, but what's a third cousin? And "twice removed?" What's that mean? Family connections can be really complicated in genealogy, so it's important to be really precise. To start, here are some handy definitions:

* First cousin—a child of your aunt or uncle.

* Second cousin—a family member who shares great-grandparents with you, but not the same grandparents.

* Third and fourth cousins—third cousins share great-

great-grandparents; fourth cousins share great-great-great grandparents, and . . . well, you get the idea.

"Removed" means that the two people involved are not the same generation. For example, you and your first cousins are in the same generation, probably both about the same age. A cousin is "once removed" if that cousin is in your parents' generation. It's like moving from the children's table to the adult table at big family dinners.

FAMILY RELATIONSHIPS

Here is a chart to help you figure it out.

1. What is your relationship to the common ancestor? Find it in the row along the top of the grid.
2. What is the other person's relationship with that same common ancestor? Find it in the column down the left side.
3. Follow your row down and the other person's column across. The box where the column and the row meet in the grid tells you your relationship to that other person. For example, you are the grandchild (second column) of a common ancestor, your grandmother. You want to figure out who you are to another grandchild (second row) of that same ancestor. Match the two up on the grid! You are first cousins!

Note: In the chart opposite, G = Great.

Here's a little practice on the chart. Can you figure out these relationships?

1. You are a great-grandchild. Who are you to another great-grandchild?
2. You are a son. What relation is a great-granddaughter to you?
3. You are a great-grandchild. Who are you to a grandchild?

	You are						
Common Ancestor	son or daughter	grandchild	G-grandchild	G-G-grandchild	G-G-G-grandchild	G-G-G-G-grandchild
son/ daughter	brother or sister	nephew/ niece	grand nephew or grand niece	G-grand nephew/ niece	G-G-grand nephew/ niece	G-G-G-grand nephew/ niece
grandchild	nephew or niece	1st cousin	1st cousin once removed	1st cousin twice removed	1st cousin 3 times removed	1st cousin 4 times removed
G-grandchild	grand nephew or grand niece	1st cousin once removed	2nd cousin	2nd cousin once removed	2nd cousin twice removed	2nd cousin 3 times removed
G-G-grandchild	G-grand nephew/ niece	1st cousin twice removed	2nd cousin once removed	3rd cousin	3rd cousin once removed	3rd cousin twice removed
G-G-G-grandchild	G-G-grand nephew/ niece	1st cousin 3 times removed	2nd cousin twice removed	3rd cousin once removed	4th cousin	4th cousin once removed
G-G-G-G-grandchild	G-G-G grand nephew/ niece	1st cousin 4 times removed	2nd cousin 3 times removed	3rd cousin twice removed	1st cousin once removed	5th cousin

(Other person — left-side label for the rows)

Answer

1. A great-grandchild and a great grandchild are second cousins.
2. A great-granddaughter and a son. The granddaughter is the son's grandniece.
3. A great-grandchild and a grandchild are first cousins once removed.

   No one expects you to memorize all this. Just keep the chart handy (put in a bookmark). Once you really get into family relationships, it's a reference tool that can't be beat.

10

Windows on the Past

One good reason to look at the past is to try to predict the future. If many people in your family have had trouble with asthma, it could mean that you and future generations will too. Many diseases are passed down through the genes. This doesn't mean that just because some family members have heart disease, everyone will. Still, it is more likely to be a problem, so extra checkups would be a good idea. And, with today's better medicines and health care, illnesses that were once a death sentence are now curable.

TRACKING MEDICAL HISTORY

Diabetes, asthma, high cholesterol, heart disease: How can you find medical information of this kind about your family?

✳   A death certificate sometimes can give clues. Does it list the cause of death as heart disease or stroke? Be careful, though— older death certificates were not always right. Many would list pneumonia as the cause of death because the person exhibited symptoms pointing to the disease. But the underlying cause could actually have been cancer, or something else.

✳   You can also contact the hospital where a relative died. Hospitals have records, and they can release them to people who have authorization. You (or your parents) will have to complete some paperwork, but it may be worth it!

✳ Relatives can sometimes provide answers. Your uncle may remember that your grandmother had terrible headaches or had to watch the sugar she ate, which could indicate diabetes.

✳ Obituaries can also give clues, too. If cause of death is not mentioned, a suggestion to send donations to an organization such as the Diabetes Foundation or American Heart Association would indicate what health problem that person had.

You should know that the names of many diseases have changed over time. If your great-grandmother tells you a great-uncle had consumption, you may not have a clue what she's talking about. But you might if she called it what it is known as today: TB (short for tuberculosis).

MATCH THE ILLNESS

Here is a list of health problems from years past. They're still around today, but with different names. See if you can match the old names with what they're called today, then check out your answers on the next page

Years Past		Today
Apoplexy	___	a. heart failure
Dropsy	___	b. typhus
Glandular fever	___	c. tonsillitis
Grippe	___	d. mononucleosis
Jail fever	___	e. pneumonia
Lockjaw	___	f. flu
Quincy	___	g. stroke
Lung fever	___	h. tetanus

Answers

Apoplexy	_g_	stroke
Dropsy	_a_	heart failure
Glandular fever	_d_	mononucleosis
Grippe	_f_	flu
Jail fever	_b_	typhus
Lockjaw	_h_	tetanus
Quincy	_c_	tonsillitis
Lung fever	_e_	pneumonia

WORDS, LIKE FASHIONS, ALSO GO OUT OF DATE

When reading or hearing family stories, you may come across other words you don't recognize. Usually you can figure out the meaning of a word from the words surrounding it. Sometimes, it's a word you think you know, but it doesn't seem to mean what you think it does. You're at a total loss!

Don't be afraid to ask questions. Sometimes the meanings of words change, and some words can mean several things. It helps to try to look up strange words in a dictionary. Even slang words can be found there. Learning slang from the past is also a part of the fun of discovering your family's world.

FAMILY SLANG DICTIONARY

Do you use slang words when talking to friends? Well, believe it or not your parents and their parents did, too. No wonder people of different generations don't always understand each other! Why not make a dictionary of slang words that were popular when your parents and grandparents were growing up?

WHAT YOU NEED

✳ small notebook ✳ pen or pencil

✳ Your computer (to store the information)

WHAT TO DO

1. Talk to your grandparents. Make up a list of words or phrases that they used to say. Write the words (along with what they mean, and how they were used) in the little notebook. Some words or phrases might be "the cat's pajamas," or "groovy" or "rad," all of which mean "great." Mark those pages as words your grandparents used.

2. Now it's your parents' turn. Ask them what slang words they used to use. Write down the words or phrases on their pages along with the meanings.

3. Finally, add your own slang words to the notebook and what you mean when you say them. Transfer the lists to the proper files on your computer or pages in your workbook, too.

4. Now, look through the pages of your family slang dictionary with your parents and grandparents (and uncles and aunts, and cousins of all ages) when the family gets together. What a great way to learn to understand each other better! And someday, when future generations look at the book, they will know how to speak your "slanguage," too.

11

The Geography of Genealogy

Where did your family come from? Where did they settle? Where did they move to after that? Maps can often point you in the right direction.

Old and new maps can help you track down information about your family. Actual birth, death, and property records are usually kept in state or county offices. If you have a general idea where a relative lived, a map of the area may confirm the name of the county and where records about the people who lived there may be kept. These archived records can provide all sorts of terrific information.

But don't rush off to find the latest, most complete map. Place names have been known to change over the years. A map dating back to when your relative was alive is likely to be of more help. It would show the old, possibly original name of towns and their boundaries back then. In early America, the boundary lines of townships and even states were flexible. You don't want to waste time researching a relative who, according to some record, lived in Connecticut, only to find out that the area was then a part of Rhode Island. State lines now are pretty much set, but county and town names, and even boundary lines, are still changed or adjusted from time to time.

What about world maps? Depending on where your ancestors are from, finding the proper map may even be more important. Over the years, countries have also changed names; for example, Ceylon to Sri Lanka (1972), Northern Rhodesia to Zambia (1964), and British Guiana to Guyana (1966). More recently,

Did you ever imagine your great-great grandmother on a camel?!

the countries that became part of the Union of Soviet Socialist Republics (USSR), or Russia, generations ago went back to their old names—or took on new ones—when the "Soviet bloc" broke up in 1989. And changes still go on today in various parts of the world; Kosovo declared independence from Serbia in 2008, and in 2016 the Czech Republic made Czechia the official shortened name in English.

Look for older maps in atlases, libraries, county or city offices, or online at historical map sites. If you can't find what you need, try looking online for information on specific place names. A search for "U.S. place names," for example, will bring you to a helpful site with free look-ups. Not only can you search and get information on just about every place name, you can click to see an aerial view of the site!

THE GEOGRAPHY TRAIL

Here's your chance to really play detective. Look for clues, those details in the maps that may bring your ancestors to life. If you know an ancestor lived somewhere near Phoenix, Arizona, look for any maps that will show you, in the greatest detail, the area where your ancestor lived. Look for locations within a county. Keep an eye out for maps that show the borders of neighboring areas. Courthouses or county offices in those areas might be good places to look for information about your relatives.

Some places are very difficult to find. It's not just that they may have changed their name. Some townships were simply too small to show up on a map. Others may have died out, becoming ghost towns that aren't on modern maps at all. That's where old maps are helpful. You can also find lists of things like abandoned post offices, which could offer important clues for you. If you know the neighborhood or street where an ancestor lived, you may find it! Try to find a map that was

Maybe some of your ancestors grew up on a farm, too.

created around the time your ancestor was alive. That's likely to be the most helpful. You can find this kind of map at local libraries or museums. Ask the librarian or historical society for help. And you can find lots of maps online. Take a look at www.oldmapsonline.org.

MAPS CAN TELL YOU

1. How your relatives lived

Maps can show you if an area was densely populated or rural, if there were many highways, or if it was mountainous. You can get an idea where your relatives were born, lived, attended school, worked, shopped, voted, traveled over land or water, raised families, and were laid to rest. Later maps of the same area might help you track down their children, and their children's children. Maybe you'll turn up some third, fourth, fifth, and sixth cousins you didn't know about.

2. What the land looked like

With certain types of maps, called "relief maps," you can see whether your relatives lived in the mountains or on hilly terrain or near small rivers or lakes. Relief maps may show conditions that would make moving or traveling to other areas difficult. Rivers that have bridges now may not have had them when your family lived nearby. Your relatives may have traveled the river by boat because it was easier than making their way on land through dense forests. Your ancestors may have even used the river to bring produce to market or go to school! Compare an old map to more modern ones, and you'll be able to see when and where new roads or bridges sprang up.

3. What your ancestors might have done for a living

If they lived near the ocean, maybe family members were fishermen. People often worked where they lived, so consider each bit of information you uncover a valuable clue, and go from there. Turning up relatives in a mining town probably meant that they worked in the mines. If you think an ancestor who lived in a heavily wooded area in Oregon in the early 1900s was a logger, and you haven't yet searched census records, why not try an online search for "Oregon loggers 1900s"? Maybe you'll discover some interesting information about him there.

4. What your ancestors did for fun

Maps can give tantalizing clues. Maybe your kin slid down grassy or snowy slopes on makeshift sleds, hiked or explored inviting caves in nearby hills, hunted in the woods, or swam in surrounding lakes. A special occasion may have meant a trip to town to catch the latest styles, or a reason to get together for a dress-up dance party. If your ancestors lived in the middle of the prairie with no neighbors nearby, they still could have read or made music and sung and laughed together. And at night, they might have sat outside and pointed out pictures they imagined in the stars.

WHAT'S IN A (PLACE) NAME?

Many place names are similar or even the same (the U.S. has about eighty-five places called Springfield). This can make your work harder. Even if a relative mentions that his grandmother lived in Tioga County, it doesn't mean it's Tioga County, New York. There's also a Tioga County in Pennsylvania. New Jersey alone has four different places called Washington. Which is the one where an ancestor lived?

When faced with place names, you'll need specifics and will need to dig deeper. Use any clues you may find. Maybe one of those four places was on a rocky hillside while another bordered a lake. If an ancestor wrote in her diary, "Went swimming again this morning. I'm so happy we live near a lake!" you can smile— you've probably found the correct Washington; but check out the other two, just in case. Pulling clues together and making connections is what makes you a good detective.

FAMILY MOVEMENT MAP

So future generations can see who lived where, why not map your family's movements? You can do this online with a digital map program, if you like, or you can make something to hang on your walls! When you're done, photos of the map can be tucked away for safekeeping in your big family scrapbook. Be sure to make extras. Family members will certainly be asking for copies of their own.

WHAT YOU NEED:

* map of the world or the country your family primarily lived in

* copies of photographs

* yarn or string

* scissors

* clear removable tape or pushpins

WHAT TO DO:

1. Spread out the map and hang it on the wall.

2. Using clear tape, affix a small photo (or photo copies) on the map where each family member lives (or lived).

3. Using a section of yarn, connect the children of a family to their parents. For example, if your great-grandparents lived in Utah, but their son moved with his family to Maine, attach a strip of yarn connecting the photo of the grandparents in Utah to the son and his family in Maine. If your family is more spread out, you can connect parents who live in Hong Kong with their five children: a son in Los Angeles, another in Sydney, Australia, and daughters in a suburb of Paris, one in Boston, and the youngest in Boulder, Colorado.

12

Family History Stories

Have you heard the one about how your great-uncle Tom gobbled sixteen blueberry pies at a pie-eating contest and then went home and ate a full dinner? Does everyone still laugh about how Grandma Ida Marie ran off and became a trapeze artist, then surprised everyone by becoming the toast of the town? Why do you think stories like these are repeated over and over? It's not just because they're such great stories. It's because they reveal as much about the person as a great photograph can.

Family stories can be about people doing everyday things, about being part of great historical events, or simply about places they've been and things they've seen. Such stories are just as much family heirlooms as a prized old pocket watch or a carefully preserved wedding dress.

THE STORYTELLING TRADITION

Stories from the past can still affect our lives today. Here's one about an immigrant who arrived at Ellis Island about a hundred years ago. At the time, doctors there examined everyone. If someone was sick, the doctor chalked an X on the back of the person's coat. Immigrants marked with an X would be held for a short time on the island to see if they got better. If they didn't, they were sent back home. It was a terrible thing for people who had left everything, looking for freedom and better lives in America, to be turned away.

Clothing styles and city brownstones help to date and place a picture.

One day, a doctor listened to an immigrant's breathing sounds. He didn't like what he heard so he quickly chalked an X on the man's back. The man knew what that meant. In a panic, he looked out across the water at the land he was so desperate to reach. Suddenly, he turned and ran, then dived straight into the water, swimming toward shore.

By the time he made it ashore, the police were waiting and easily took the exhausted man into custody. He was brought to court, but the judge hearing the story was more amazed than angry.

"If you're healthy enough to swim that distance, you're certainly healthy enough to make it here," he said. Then he made it official—"You can stay."

The story is a true one—part of the family history of a friend of mine. Anytime anyone in the family was about to give up on something they truly wanted, the story of the grandfather who swam to shore was retold. The message was: if your grandfather could overcome great odds, so can you! It made my friend proud. And it made her feel that, just like her grandfather, she could do anything if she set her mind to it.

Family stories knit generations together. They can encourage, console, or sometimes just spark laughter. And they can make you feel closer to your ancestors.

MORE THAN A STORY

Family stories can also provide clues to help you find more information about your family. As part of a story, someone might mention the name of the town where a relative you've been searching for used to live. A story about great-grandma's prize quilt might lead you to a quilting organization with lists of present and past members online.

The collecting of family stories is sometimes called taking "oral histories," because they are verbal records of a time and a place. All this can help you in your genealogical research. You've read about World War II in your history books, but imagine how much more alive that dry information will be if you hear about it from someone who actually lived through it—someone related to you!

What will you do with these family stories? Besides helping you in your research, you may want to write out some of them and include them in your family scrapbook. For example, in Grandma's section, you might want to include the story about how she met Grandpa. Or you can copy down all the stories and put them together in their own separate book. A great thing to do is to gather your relatives and use a camera or phone to film them telling the stories. That way, you can capture their expressions and their joy! Then make copies or put the whole thing on CDs to give to family members.

TAKING ORAL HISTORIES

There's an art to collecting family stories. Once you have the tools: pencils, notebook, your phone or a voice recorder, the first thing you'll need to do is know how to listen. Give all your attention to the storyteller and don't interrupt. Save your questions for the end. Don't rush the speaker or criticize. How would you feel if you were telling a story and someone said, "Could you tell the story a little faster?" or "This part is boring, can we skip it and get to the good parts?" Instead, say things like, "This is fascinating!" or "I could listen forever!" with an interested look on your face. It's a sure way to get the storyteller to answer your follow-up questions and want to tell you more.

MAKE UP A LIST OF QUESTIONS

Don't put anyone on the spot by asking them to "Tell me a story about your life." Prepare a list of questions to help start things off. And don't forget a notebook or tape recorder to record their answers.

Here are a few starter or follow-up questions you may want to ask:

Places
1. Where did you grow up?
2. What was your house like?
3. Where did you buy your clothes and shop for food?

4. What did you do for fun where you lived?

5. Did you travel? Where? What did you see?

People

1. What were your parents like?

2. Do you remember your teachers?

3. Who did you admire most when you were growing up?

4. Who played a part in changing your life?

5. Who was the first person you fell in love with? Can you talk about the person?

In Those Days

1. Can you tell me about when you first moved here?

2. What kind of work did you and other family members do?

3. What was going on in the world?

4. How did what happened affect you and the family?

5. How has life changed for you since then?

Emotions

1. What story about yourself or your family makes you smile?

2. What story about yourself or your family makes you laugh?

3. What story about yourself or your family makes you cry?

4. What story about yourself or your family makes you wonder about things?

5. What story about yourself or your family makes you feel proud?

WHAT'S *YOUR* STORY?

You're part of your family tree, too. So don't forget to write down your own stories. They will be memories that you can hand down to future generations. Keep them, and any other family stories, in your loose-leaf workbook or put them in the family scrapbook.

Car models can help date photographs—early ones had running boards.

13

The Way They Were

WERE THE GOOD OLD DAYS REALLY SO GOOD?

Grandparents, and their grandparents, might have mentioned or talked at length about how much better things were in "the old days." Their memories might have softened over time—because life in the "good old days" wasn't always easy. For example:

* Frontier women did laundry by putting it in washtubs and stamping on it with their feet, pounding it with rocks on a riverbank, or scrubbing it against a washboard.
* Until as late as 1860, pigs were free to roam urban American streets. This was encouraged because they would eat the garbage left strewn all over the roads.
* Federal child labor laws were passed in 1938. Before that, children often were made to work twelve to fifteen hours a day in factories. If they got hurt or couldn't work, they were quickly replaced by others who could. Before 1900, a third of all mill hands were children.
* In the 1960s, women couldn't open up a checking account without a husband co-signing for them.

✳ Women were banned from attending certain colleges, like Princeton, which finally opened its doors to women in 1969.

Think back to what life was like fifty or a hundred years ago. In the 1950s, families felt most modern when they ate convenient canned food or frozen TV dinners. Most didn't want the trouble of fresh vegetables and fruits. But nowadays, we know that fresh is best. My, how times change!

What about life today do you think could stand improvement? Imagine how things might be in the future. For example, do you hate having to take a daily vitamin? Some day, there might be a type of "vitamin pill" given to you at birth that would take care of all your vitamin needs for your entire life!

WRITE A LETTER TO THE PAST

Pick one of your ancestors and write that person a letter. What would you say to your great-great-grandfather who came over from Poland? What would you tell him about yourself? What would you want to ask him? What do you think he would say to you?

BE A GREAT-GREAT-GREAT FOR A DAY!

A few years back several so-called "reality" shows were aired on TV with families or groups of strangers living as pioneers did hundreds of years ago. They had no running water, no electricity. They wore the same kinds of clothes and used the same tools as the pioneers did, and they grew crops and ate the same food as in "the old days." To make things even more authentic, some were given a list of rules to follow, based on those the pioneers lived under so long ago.

Even if you didn't see these shows, you can still imagine what life was like. Think about what you have now that they didn't. Start with running water; and not only running water but hot and cold running water!

But back then . . . You open your eyes and try to wake up. There's no running water, but you might splash your face from a basin of cold water (of course, in winter you would first have to break the film of ice covering it)! No indoor plumbing, so you know what a hassle it would be dealing with that! And forget taking a real bath or a shower.

Now, what was life like for your great-grandparents and grandparents? Your grandparents were probably around your age in the 1950s or '60s. Your great-grandparents were most likely around your age in the 1930s. That's not as long ago as pioneer days, but what do you suppose they had at your age?

* Ball point pens.
* Rotary telephones—landlines only; definitely no wifi or cell phones!
* Radio programs (think TV drama, sit-coms, concerts without a picture). There was no Internet radio or podcasts.
* Record players played 78 rpm (revolutions per minute) vinyl records with one song on each side, then albums at 45 and 33⅓ rpm. No music-to-go, available 24/7.

* You went out to the movies. There were no DVDs to bring the theater experience right into your home.
* No SUVs.
* Black-and-white TV, then color; no flat, wide, and hang-on-your-wall or 3D screens with news instantly "beamed in" from around the world.
* Manual, then electric typewriters; now, computers and printers, digital cameras, even cell phones and watches that act as computers, all unknown to your great-grandparents in "their day," are there for you today.

In the kitchen, your great-grandmother's grandmother probably had a wood- or oil-burning stove and an "ice-box" to keep things cold (the melting ice collected in a pan underneath and would overflow if she didn't empty it in time). For entertainment, books were always around, but forget computer games. Games were a deck of cards or were on boards and meant for two (chess, checkers) or a whole family to play together. Early TV had only a few channels, and programs were on for only a few hours a day. The shows were broadcast live. If someone made a mistake or something unexpected happened (think *America's Funniest Home Videos*) everyone who was tuned in saw it! No hundred channels coming into your home by cable or bounced off satellites! No pictures sent back from cameras launched into space or "rovered" around on nearby planets.

Girls, you might not have been deciding what you wanted to be when you grow up. You might have been expected to marry and stay home, keeping house and taking care of your family while your husband went out to work. Your days would be spent cooking, washing, ironing, and sewing. Of course, many of those things are still done today, but timesaving devices (washer/dryers, microwave ovens) have made things a lot easier. Boys, you might not have had much of a choice in your career, either—if your family owned a farm or a business, you might have been to carry it on. Now, people have the chance to decide for themselves what they want to do with their lives and see how far they can go—whether it's to win a gold medal at the Olympics, be the first one in the family to get a Ph.D., or fly to Mars.

Yes, things have changed a lot over the years from your great-grandmother to you. Can you even imagine what things your grandchildren will see when you reach the age your grandmother is now? What will the world be like in your children's future?

Things are constantly changing, and it's hard to imagine what effect these changes had on your ancestors and older family members. Sometimes, to understand things, it helps to see them. Since your family stretches back through time, you can get a better picture of their life changes by making a genealogical timeline.

GENEALOGICAL TIMELINE

WHAT YOU NEED

* photographs, news clippings, historical items
* lightweight clothesline or twine
* small paper clips
* yarn or ribbon of different colors
* stick-on labels

WHAT TO DO

1. Gather some family photos or make copies. You'll want pictures of your grandparents from babyhood to the present,

of your parents, and of yourself, too. Look for house photos: the one your great-grandparents lived in, the one your grandparents lived in and, finally, the house you live in now. If you want more, consider photos of family pets through the years, the cars your family owned, groups at special occasions, even favorite toys.

2. Put all the pictures in order chronologically, the oldest ones first.

3. Use tape to put up a length of clothesline, twine, or ribbon so it stretches across a wall. This is your basic timeline.

4. Divide the timeline into time periods by tying and hanging down some yarn or ribbon to represent time periods of ten, twenty-five, or fifty years. Tie them loosely so that space can be adjusted based on the number of photographs you want to hang.

5. To make the timeline's years easier to see, write the time periods (1920s, for example) on labels and attach them to the hanging markers.

6. Clip each photo from the pile onto the timeline, starting at the left: Your grandfather as a young boy. The year he was twenty-two. Your mom when she was five, and when she got married. Adjust the positions and time period markers as you go to fill the timeline with photographs.

7. If there's room, add historical information such as special dates, illustrations, and clippings from books. For example, if a relative fought in World War II, attach copies of photographs or newspaper items about the war in that space on the timeline.

What did they do before these popular inventions? Ask your parents, grandparents, and great-grandparents:

ballpoint pen	1938
Band-Aids	1920
bubble gum	1928
cell phone	1980s
credit card	1950
crossword puzzle	1913
disposable contact lenses	1980
The Internet	1990s
jet engine	1930
Post-it notes	1974
roller blades	1979
teabag	1904
3D movies	1922
TV remote control	1950
zipper	1913

14

Family Traditions

A tradition can be anything from going to the beach every summer to always saying "bunny, bunny, bunny" for good luck when you wake up. What traditions have been handed down in your family?

If your family has a tradition of eating dinner together, it's a great chance for everyone to talk over what happened during the day, or to air out problems. One friend of mine grew up with family night; her father would read something aloud and the family would discuss it and use it to generate more conversation. Another family had game night. They would pull out a favorite board game, put out bowls of snacks, and sit around the table and play. What would be a great activity for your family to do every week? Go bowling? Cook dinner together?

If you do start a new family tradition, maybe it will still be going strong when your grandchildren are your age.

CELEBRATION TIME!

What holidays does your family celebrate? Whatever your religion or personal beliefs, the calendar is full of special days and opportunities for celebrating—and for starting new traditions.

The birthday cake with candles was a new tradition a little over two hundred years ago. It started in Germany as a cake of sweetened bread dough. When the candles were blown out, the smoke would carry birthday wishes up to the gods.

Why not come up with your own family reason for celebrating, and schedule it every year on a certain date. It could be as simple as, every spring, planting marigolds in a small portion of your backyard to celebrate new life. The choices are as open as your imagination!

TRADITIONAL FOODS

Certain foods are traditional for special holidays: hamantaschen, cookies shaped like three-cornered hats, celebrate the Jewish holiday of Purim. Christmas cookies are often flat shapes decorated with red and green sugar. And what's Thanksgiving without turkey and cranberry sauce and all the fixings? Countries around the world have traditional foods for holidays and family meals. In the U.S., favorite foods can even vary from state to state. Your relatives in North Carolina might love their barbecue, while your relatives in Boston might be more interested in baked beans and cream pie.

HOME COOKING?

"It's just like Mom used to make." How many times have you heard someone say that? Yes, holidays are good reasons for extra-special meals, and old-fashioned home cooking often deserves the highest praise any meal can get! It means food that's cooked with love and care. And special recipes often have secret ingredients and are handed down from generation to generation. It's a great way to keep a strong connection with your ancestors. Make your great great-great grandmother's recipe for stuffed cabbage the way she did, and you are re-creating a part of your past!

Back when people didn't have cookbooks or the Internet to look for recipes, they wrote them down and handed them out, often on index cards, as gifts along with a tray or taste of the recipe. My mother's recipe cards were often faded and worn from use. We looked forward to those family favorites. Why not make your own recipe box and stock it with your family's favorite recipes? Or use an app to create a virtual recipe box with digital index cards. You don't even need to print anything.

Collect every recipe you can find that has been handed down by family members (ask if they have more) and make a special family recipe box to hold them. Or use your digital cards and upload them to the genealogy pages you're creating. (First make sure you have permission to share the recipes so openly and freely, of course.) With a little research, you may even find recipes that an ancestor might have enjoyed. Then title them with zingy names such as Aunt Martha's Marvelous Munchy Candy Mounds, Uncle Bob's Spicy-Licious Barbeque Sauce, or Cousin Irma's Devilishly Delicious Devil's Food Cake.

RECIPE BOX

When you're in a mood to cook, it's great to have your family's favorite recipes all in the same place. So now's the time to get started on this kitchen project.

WHAT YOU NEED

* Your family recipes!
* photo storage box or shoe box
* tempera paint
* magazine clippings of anything to do with food. (Cut out pictures, and even lettering, to decorate your box with "Good Eating!" or "What's Cooking?")
* white glue
* scissors
* plastic dish
* soft brush
* index cards in different colors

WHAT TO DO

1. First, paint the box a bright color. Be sure to let it dry completely!

2. Select pictures and lettering, and decide on a pattern.

3. Pour some glue into a plastic dish. Use a soft brush to apply the glue to the back of your paper cutouts and affix them to the box.

4. After the glue has dried completely, apply a thin layer of glue all over the box.

5. While the box is drying, copy the recipes or glue photocopies of them to the index cards—longer recipes onto both front and back of a card, or onto the front of two or more cards that you then staple together. (If you're hand-writing the recipes, select pastel cards or you might not be able to read the instructions.)

6. Put the cards in the box.

FUN FACTS

* Apples have been around for many years, but applesauce wasn't invented commercially until 1390.

* The first potato chips (fried potatoes cut "thin") were made in 1853.

* It was at the 1904 World's Fair in St. Louis that ice cream and waffles were brought together—and the ice-cream cone was born.

* None of your relatives tasted Jell-O® before 1910. That's when the quivering dessert was first invented.

FAMILY SONGS

In the Appalachian Mountains, there is a tradition called "song catching." Long before the invention and popular use of tape recorders, people would "catch" songs.

They were sung over and over until someone younger than the singer memorized them. In this way, their songs were passed down from generation to generation, in much the same way oral histories were transmitted. Of course, as people took turns singing the songs, they sometimes changed them. A young woman with a nice soprano voice might have added some high trills, while an expert banjo player put in extra chords and harmonies. One singer probably sang a tune slowly or softly, while another sang out gleefully. It may have been the same song, but many people interpreted it and many different versions arose.

Historical events also lead to other kinds of songs. During World War II everybody in the U.S., including your relatives, was probably singing along to the morale-building "Boogie Woogie Bugle Boy from Company B," made famous by the Andrews Sisters. Another song, dating from the Revolutionary War, is still known today as "Yankee Doodle." The song was actually British in origin, making fun of colonists as know-nothing bumpkins! Instead of getting upset, the colonists took on the song as their own and sang it with pride. What songs do you suppose your ancestors sang, and what did the songs mean to them? Ask your older family members to sing some traditional songs that they remember from their childhood. Maybe you can "catch" them or record some of the traditional songs of earlier generations.

Bathing suits covered much more than many suits do today.

RECORD SOME FAVORITES

Get in tune with the songs that have been enjoyed by family members over the years. Does your mom sing along so often to those "old" folk tunes her mother loved to sing, you've learned the words, too? Does your granddad suddenly stop talking to listen intently whenever he recognizes the great tenor voice of Pavarotti on a classical radio station? Maybe jazz, hip-hop, big band, rock-and-roll, or today's pop music is always playing in some room of your house or through private earphones. If everybody marches to the beat of a different drummer, why not do some research and make up a "sampler" of favorites? Include something for everybody, from your mom and dad's special song that they danced to at their wedding to the tune that your grandma sings softly whenever she is sitting with a new grandchild. Set the music playing at your next family barbecue or get-together, and you'll probably hear Grandpa Garcia, or Aunt Dorothy, or cousin Angelo say, "Listen, that's my favorite song." It's certainly something you'll want to keep, to remember everyone by for years to come.

15

A Family Reunion!

Now that you've gotten to know your whole family better, why not celebrate by helping them all get to know one another better, too? The best way to do this is with a family reunion. When's the last time you got together with your family? Thanksgiving? New Year's Eve? When was the last time you saw all your family—aunts, cousins, nephews, and second and third—and even fourth—cousins, too? A year ago at your Aunt Ray's wedding? Two years ago? Some families have yearly family gatherings where hundreds of members come together for picnics or parties.

Whether you make it a yearly event or a once-in-a-lifetime celebration, having a reunion is a great way for family members to keep in touch. And what's more fun than a party? Although there's a lot you can do on your own, you're going to need the help of your parents for this.

First, what kind of party should you have? Give it some thought. A big picnic in the park? A barbecue in the backyard? Or will you need to rent a hall someplace? What is decided, assuming your parents sign on to the idea, will depend on the size of your family, the cost, when the reunion is scheduled, and what kind of things your family enjoys. Are you all beachlovers? Or do you enjoy dressing up for formal occasions? Do the relatives like jazz or classical music, or would they prefer quiet? Does your family quickly line up for hotdogs and burgers from a grill or prefer to sit down to a meal? Should you hire a DJ or live band, or can family members provide their own musical entertainment? These are all things to take into consideration.

TIME TO SEND OUT INVITATIONS

You've gotten a go for the party! Good! Now, start by making up a list of those to be invited. Run it by your parents, because you don't want to forget anyone. Some family members may live across the country or even halfway around the world. Some may have other things scheduled, so can't come. Still, they should be invited—and you might be pleasantly surprised to see them turn up or prepare something on their own to join in the family fun!

FAMILY REUNION INVITATION

With many people to invite, it's a good idea to design and print your own invitations. It's easy to do this on a computer, and you can even send out the invitations as e-vites and save on the postage! Check out www.evite.com, or paperlesspost.com.

If not, it is perfectly fine to design a simple single-sheet invitation and photocopy it in black and white or color.

WHAT YOU NEED
* paper
* pens
* markers

* clippings
* access to photocopier
* envelopes to fit

WHAT TO DO

1. First, decide what you want your invitation to look like. The cover could say something as simple as YOU'RE INVITED!

2. If you have any scans of family photos, you could include one or more on a single sheet. Alternatively, you can use drawings or glued-on art if you're doing the invitations by hand.

3. Next, you want to give the event a name (The First Annual Hodgson Family Reunion!), tell them where it will be (The Riverdale Country Club, 444 Madison Lane, Boston, Mass.), and when it will be (1 pm to 4 pm, Saturday, June 4, 2018).

4. Add a line suggesting what family members might bring, such as: Bring yourselves, your favorite stories, a family potluck with recipe. Bring special photographs and significant objects and other memorabilia to share.

5. Print the letters RSVP and your phone number. RSVP stands for the French "Repondez s'il vous plait," meaning that it asks people to call and let you know if they will be coming or not.

Once the invitation is finished, you're ready to have as many invitations printed as you need. Then all you have to do is prepare the envelopes and get them in the mail.

A REAL FAMILY MEAL

Remember when you were collecting all those recipes for your recipe box and cookbook? Now is the time to ask family members who will be coming to prepare a family heirloom recipe for the potluck and bring it to share. Check with them to see what they will be able to bring. You want to have a good selection of food, especially if certain family members have food allergies or need special diets. Make a list to see if you need any other main dishes, sides, salads, or desserts. If you do, check your family recipe box for something you would like to contribute. If you're not an experienced cook, trying something new can be challenging. Don't be afraid to ask your parents for help. After all, they're family, too!

DECK THE HALLS!

To get things started, have a table set up where people can put the significant objects they brought with them: Great-Aunt Ethel's first pair of roller skates, which came with a skate key! The cloth doll Great-Grandmother handed down to Aunt Takako. Your own first pair of baby shoes! As people arrive, they can put their interesting treasures on the table.

AND HERE'S . . . THE FAMILY!

Bring out the results of your family research and get ready for smiles. Remember, if you have all your information on your computer, you can simply print it all out and make copies for everyone. You could also share things as a slideshow or PowerPoint!

Here are some things to share:

* Your genealogy timeline—if you can't move it out of your room for the great day, you'll just have to clean your room and invite everyone in.

* Your own family tree and genealogy loose-leaf binder; it's a good time for relatives to check names, dates, and facts. You'd be surprised how many misspellings are discovered—and can be corrected—when people examine documents and check them. If you made the family tree on a computer, you can print it out and bring it along. Keep a small notebook and pencil handy to record any details that need to be changed or followed up on.

* Your traditional and "sampler" music, and some music on your phone from the different decades (your parents probably have some put aside); anybody want to sing along?

* Your oral history recordings, along with written copies of favorite family stories; maybe they'll inspire a few other family members to tell stories of their own.

* Your family recipe box with favorite recipes; did anyone bring new old favorites?

* Your family scrapbook; by now you should have many pages in it, filled with photos, recipes, and facts, facts, facts. You may want to print the scrapbook from your computer, too! Or burn it onto CDs and give them out as keepsakes.

FAMILY PHOTO SPOT

You'll want to have a place where your reunion guests can enjoy looking over some family photos—and maybe add a few of their own. Maybe you can move your genealogy timeline from

your room to the living room and leave space underneath it for another line to hold photos brought by family members. If that doesn't work, put up a single line, or some shorter ones, to hang guests' photos. Attach a few pictures to start, and also to show what the lines are for, then leave a basket nearby with clips for your guests to use.

If there's no room for lines of photographs, set up a few cork bulletin boards. Keep pushpins handy for people to tack up any photos they brought. (If you place a pushpin at the top edge of a photo and another at the bottom edge, you can hold a photo in place without having to puncture the photograph itself.) Have stick-on labels, pens, and markers available, and encourage your guests to label their photos and identify the people in them and the locations.

LET THE FESTIVITIES BEGIN!

People coming to the reunion will bring their photos or tell stories about the people and places that mean something special to them, like the covered bridge where Grandpa proposed to Grandma! Big sister might bring her favorite Barbie, the one she got when she was six. Compare and contrast! How much have things changed? How have they stayed the same? Bring your treasures and memorabilia, too. It's show-and-tell time for everyone!

For "who's who" fun, post a variety of pictures on a bulletin board and, underneath, reveal who it is a picture of and when the photo was taken. Keep pictures of close family members together, so people can see who looks like whom. Be sure to have a group of "you must have been a beautiful baby" shots, with photos nearby of the same people as adults. See if everyone can match the baby pictures with the grown-ups.

WE'VE GOT GAMES!

Make sure you have plenty of things to do to keep the party rolling. One activity is to get everyone together for a "when I was a girl/when I was a boy" game. It's more fun when relatives of all ages (great-grandma to just-turned-teen) play. For this game, you need to prepare in advance a dozen or more slips of paper with a question written on each and place them in a bowl. Each person is asked to select a paper from the bowl, think back to when they were between eight and twelve years old, and answer the question. Other people playing the game can chime in

with their answers and comments—but they still have to select a paper when it's their turn!

Here are some questions and requests to start you off. Add more of your own if you wish, but it's best to keep things general. You don't want to embarrass anyone.

* Who was really, really famous then and why?
* What was your favorite candy?
* What did you really love to wear?
* Sing the first two lines of your favorite song.
* Where did you like to go on summer vacations?
* What games did you like to play?
* What kind of pet did you have and why?
* What gift did you receive that was special?
* What movie did you go to see several times?
* Recite something that you learned in school.
* Who was president, and what was happening in the world?
* What TV or radio show did you always listen to?
* What was your favorite meal?
* When you went out, what was it you did?
* What happened to you that seems funny to you now, but maybe wasn't then?

REMEMBER FAMILY PHOTOS!

Don't forget to take video the event and have others take video of it, too. It's easy to use your phone to do this!

Let each guest say a few words for the camera or phone: Who they are. Where they're from. What family means to them. If you have your notebook handy, you might want to jot down a word or two to remind you to follow up on something. But don't try to write everything down, you won't have time. And you want to enjoy the family reunion, too!

Don't forget to take several group photos of the whole entire clan! That's super important! If you have a big family, gather everyone outside, provided the weather is reasonable, and get everyone in place—some people may need to sit or kneel in front. (Ask if everyone can see the camera.) Maybe you can have a photographer come by, or a neighbor who is handy with a camera can take few shots—and a few more "just in case"—so nobody in the family will be left out of these very special photos. As long as you have a camera handy, consider some sibling or cousin photos of the older generations, with people arranged by birth order.

Keeping in Touch

Just because the reunion is over, doesn't mean the good times have to stop. There are lots of ways you can still keep in touch and share! Treasure your First Annual Family Reunion by gathering photos and preserving all those terrific memories for the next family get-together. Find the best photo of the whole family. Scan it onto thank-you cards, or have copies of the photo made to send to everyone. Photos can also be sent to those who didn't come—maybe next year, they'll be the first to arrive for the fun!

START A FAMILY NEWSLETTER

In the meantime, a newsletter is a great way for a family to keep in touch and share news. You can take your list of all the people you invited to the reunion, including the ones who weren't able to come, and turn it into a newsletter mailing list or send it out via email. When would you send out your newsletter? Maybe once a year at holiday time? Midway between family reunions? Maybe even twice a year, six months apart? What will you call the newsletter? How about *The Family Bugle*?

The most important details are: What is the newsletter going to say? How will you get the "news" for the newsletter?

Before you even begin to put together that first issue, email a brief note to everyone telling them that you are starting a family newsletter. Ask that whenever they have news to report or have family photos, to contact you! Tell them that you'd like to know things such as:

* Did anything special happen recently?
* How has the year been for you?
* What were the good things that happened?
* Did any bad things happen that you want to talk about?
* If you go to work, did anything interesting happen on the job?
* If you are in school, what are you studying?
* What films did you see this year? Which ones did you especially like?
* What books did you read this year? What was your favorite and why?
* Did you watch any sports? Which teams do you root for?

Gather up all the responses, put them in a folder, and refer to them when you write the text of your newsletter. Try to include as many different relatives in each issue of the newsletter as you can—so that they can look forward to mentions of themselves as well as to catching up on the news about other family members.

Next, you have to decide what your newsletter will look like. Not all of your relatives, especially the much older ones, will have access to a computer. Will it be a handwritten sheet that you photocopy, or something created on your computer and that you print on special paper, or will it be a file you send by email? Do you want to include photographs? Do you want a "Good News" section? Do you want to share recipes? How about information on favorite travel spots? Maybe you want to add some original poems and stories, too. And don't forget items about the last family reunion or reminders about the next one you might be planning!

LAUNCH A FAMILY WEBSITE

Whatever you can do with a newsletter, you can do on a website. With your family's permission and help, the right computer software, and some technical know-how, you might be able to get a website up and running yourself. If not, books are available to tell you what to do and how to do it, and some websites can help you set one up—or set it up for you. A website can be as creative and unique as you like, with photographs in full color, and even short videos or animation. Since websites can be accessed all over the world, family members don't have to live right next door anymore, or down the block, or even in the next township over. People can live anywhere around the world and still be close!

Lucky you, if a sign tells where a photo was taken.

And you thought great grandpa only used a cane as he got older!

17

Back to the Future

It's been fun, and through genealogy, you've gotten to know your whole family better, maybe going back to long before you were born. Now, what would you like family members still to come—your children, your children's children, and great- and grandnephews and nieces—to know about you? Why not put together a personal time capsule? You can leave them all a unique message that says, "Hello!" What better way is there to bring together your whole family—past, present, and future?

A "MY TIME" CAPSULE

The hardest part of a time capsule is deciding what to put inside. But whatever you do, don't forget to include copies of your family tree research. You'll be saving your descendants from having to do all that information gathering all over again.

WHAT YOU NEED:

* a container (coffee can, cookie tin, small box, plastic bag, or wrapping)

* markers   * items that say "my time"

* a safe place

What do you think your great-great grandkids would want to know about you and your time? What will you put into your time capsule?

1. PHOTOS: Put together a small photo album showing your family at work and play—how they live and dress. Label or caption each photo with the person's name and the date the photo was taken, and where. Remember to include pictures of yourself, your friends, your room—after all, this is your capsule!

2. CLOTHING: What are the latest styles? Put in a pair of your favorite shoes or the jeans that you've just outgrown. Show you're a fan—include a baseball cap with the name of your favorite team.

3. TECHNOLOGY: Tuck in some kinetic sand or some Lego architecture pieces. Cut out ads with prices for other "wish list" items—in the far future, they may not even be a memory.

4. FOOD: Avoid treating generations of ants to your favorite candy bar—a neatly flattened wrapper or two will do. What do you like to eat? Include a list in the time capsule. Maybe the finder of your time capsule will have the same taste in food.

5. NEWSPAPERS: Today's headlines! Newspaper decays, so protect paper items in heavy plastic, or laminate clippings that mean something special to you and your family.

MORE STUFF
FOR YOUR TIME CAPSULE

Want to get closer to your family to come? Maybe someday you'll sit in a rocker and tell your grandkids stories about when you were their age. Maybe even your great-grandchildren. But your time capsule may not be found until after you're gone, and you're living now. So, here's your chance. Write a letter to those future generations.

HERE'S AN EXAMPLE:

Dear great-great-great-great-grandchildren,
My name is Elaine. It's 2017 and I'm eleven.
Living in Boston is lots of fun because there's so much to do: museums and shopping and movies and just hanging out and playing Frisbee in the Boston Common. I intend to be an award-winning scientist when I grow up.

TAKING THE GRAND TOUR

In 1962, Jacqueline Kennedy, the wife of President John F. Kennedy, gave TV viewers a historic guided tour of the White House. Why not treat your grandkids, or great-great grandkids, to a guided tour of the place you call home?

Do you have a video or regular camera? You can use that, or your phone, to produce your own tour. Start from the outside of your house and work your way in. Label your photos, or write or talk about what each room is used for—here's where I beat my brother at chess. Here's where my mother writes her novels. Point out interesting facts. This is the desk where I wrote my first short story! Here's where I go when I'm in a bad mood and want to be by myself. Make the tour as personal as you'd like—it's for your family, after all.

DO NOT OPEN UNTIL . . .

Assemble everything into your time capsule. Identify it and mark it with a "Do not open until" date: twenty years into the future, thirty years, maybe fifty years. Even New Year's Eve 2100 (although you may not be around to see it)! On your genealogy page in your notebook, make a note about the time capsule (the date you made it up and where you put it) so that it is not forgotten and lost forever. Make sure that it is properly protected, and then put it away somewhere.

Where will you put your time capsule?

* In the backyard: If you bury it, draw a map to remind yourself where it is. Protect the time capsule from water and other damage by wrapping it in strong plastic bags or sheeting.
* Hidden under a staircase, or behind a loose board in a wall: Out of sight, out of mind.
* In the attic: Put it out of the way, so it isn't accidentally tossed out the next time Dad has a cleaning fit up there.
* In your closet: You can keep an eye on it there, but snoopy siblings may get curious.

A PEEK AT THE FUTURE

Just as you've discovered generations of your family going back a hundred or so years, there probably will be generations of your family going forward many years. Can you imagine that?

In *The Time Machine*, written by H. G. Wells, a man invents a machine to travel into the future. He remains in one place, sitting in the time machine in the basement of his house. Through his basement window, he can see a dummy in the window of a shop nearby. As he is "traveling," he watches the hem of the mannequin's dress get shorter, then longer, then shorter, then wider—as styles change through the years. Suddenly, the little shop window disappears—and he's there in the future!

Imagine your own home. Will it still be there in twenty years? Or fifty years? What will things be like in one hundred years? Will houses be built on the ground, under ground, or stretch way up into the sky? Will there be speedy flyers hovering around, instead of streets and long highways filled with cars?

Imagine you are all grown up. Maybe you're married. What does your wife or husband look like? What kind of work do you do? What do your kids look like? Do people tell you that your children have your same crooked smile? Do your kids have a dog or a cat like you used to at their age? Did you just remember the date you put on your time capsule? Now imagine four and five generations of your family getting together someday at reunions—one that you started!

Afterword

Plant It, It's Your Family Tree

Part of what makes genealogy so much fun is that it keeps growing and changing before your very eyes. Everything you learn about your family adds to it. Your family is a vibrant and living thing, and what better way to symbolize it than as a living and growing tree?

Go to a local nursery and ask someone there to help you select a tiny sapling that will grow well for you. Get planting and growing instructions to take with you. When you get home, plant the tree right away. You may have a nice place selected in front of your house or in your backyard. A very large pot on a porch or patio might do for a while, but a tree belongs in the ground. Its roots need room and nourishment in order to grow tall, and the branches and leaves of most trees will want to spread out. Care for your family tree and watch it grow from year to year. Every time you look at it, you'll be reminded of the wonderful living, growing thing each and everyone's family truly is.

Additional Reading

Family Tree Kids!

A genealogy website from the creators of *Family Tree Magazine*, full of activities and research tips.

kids.familytreemagazine.com

MyHeritage

You can search simultaneously across different databases here and you can also build your own digital family tree and create your own family website.

myheritage.com

The Official Federal Land Records Site

This site from the U.S. Department of the Interior contains over 5 million land title records, going all the way back to 1820. They can help you figure out when your relatives may have bought and sold land. (You can also check individual states' land record sites!)

glorecords.blm.gov

BillionGraves

It may sound morbid, but this site and app have a huge database of tombstone images. You can even upload your own photos of tombstones to help connect with possible relatives!

billiongraves.com

Chronicling America

This website from the Library of Congress provides access to select digital newspaper pages from 1836-1922. Search by state, ethnicity, or keyword to see if your family name is in print!

chroniclingamerica.loc.gov

Index

Note: Page numbers in **bold** indicate word definitions.

About the Author

CAROLINE LEAVITT is *The New York Times* and *USA Today* bestselling author of *Cruel Beautiful World* and several other adult novels. She teaches novel-writing online at both Stanford University and UCLA Extension Writers' Program and works with writers privately. Caroline has appeared on the *Today Show*, *Diane Rehm*, German and Canadian TV, and more, and she has been featured on *The View from the Bay*. She has a son, Max, who is studying acting, and she lives in Hoboken, New Jersey, with her husband, the writer Jeff Tamarkin.